Implementing
RESPONSE TO
INTERVENTION

To all the teachers and principals who have allowed me to learn with them.

To my husband, David, who is my business partner and a source of constant support, and my two amazing children, Brandon and Lauren.

A PRINCIPAL'S GUIDE

Implementing
RESPONSE TO
INTERVENTION

Susan L. Hall

Foreword by
Elaine K. McEwan

CORWIN PRESS
A SAGE Company
Thousand Oaks, CA 91320

For information:

Corwin Press
A SAGE Company
2455 Teller Road
Thousand Oaks, California 91320
www.corwinpress.com

SAGE India Pvt. Ltd.
B 1/I 1 Mohan Cooperative
    Industrial Area
Mathura Road, New Delhi 110 044
India

SAGE Ltd.
1 Oliver's Yard
55 City Road
London EC1Y 1SP
United Kingdom

SAGE Asia-Pacific Pte. Ltd.
33 Pekin Street #02-01
Far East Square
Singapore 048763

Printed in the United States of America.

Library of Congress Cataloging-in-Publication Data

Hall, Susan L. (Susan Long)
Implementing response to intervention: a principal's guide/Susan L. Hall.
    p. cm.
Includes bibliographical references and index.
ISBN 978-1-4129-5506-5 (cloth)
ISBN 978-1-4129-5507-2 (pbk.)

  1. Reading—Remedial teaching—Handbooks, manuals, etc. 2. Learning disabled children—Education—Handbooks, manuals, etc. 3. School principals—United States—Handbooks, manuals, etc. I. Title.

LB1050.5.H258 2008
372.43—dc22   2007036309

This book is printed on acid-free paper.

        08   09   10   11   10 9 8 7 6 5 4 3

Acquisitions Editor:	Robb Clouse
Editorial Assistant:	Jessica Bergmann
Production Editor:	Eric Garner
Copy Editor:	Carol Anne Peschke
Typesetter:	C&M Digitals (P) Ltd.
Proofreader:	Charlotte J. Waisner
Indexer:	Molly Hall
Cover Designer:	Rose Storey
Graphic Designer:	Lisa Miller

9/9/09

Contents

List of Tables and Figures

Tables

Figures

Foreword

Elaine K. McEwan

As I read *Implementing Response to Intervention: A Principal's Guide,* I could not help but remember the dozens of meetings I attended in my years as an elementary school principal. At the time I took the job, I knew very little about beginning reading instruction or special education. I had been a media specialist up to that point. But I did know the importance of learning to read and loving to read and was always deeply concerned about the students in our school who were failing to thrive in reading, particularly those in kindergarten and first grade. The teachers, whether classroom, special education, or reading, had a number of pat answers when we sat around the table to talk about how we could better meet the needs of these students: "They're just not ready yet. They aren't developmentally able to handle the demands of an academic curriculum. They're late bloomers." I would press the issue about getting some intensive help for a child immediately, and eyes would roll. Surely I knew that we had to wait until we could document a discrepancy between a student's ability and his or her achievement. Meanwhile, that child became frustrated, the parents were upset, and our hands were tied waiting for Matthew, Erica, and John to "bloom." "How will we know when this child is ready?" I asked. "Will he suddenly start reading spontaneously?" The teachers were not certain that I understood the intricacies of early childhood education or special education. Oh, I understood them, all right. It just didn't make sense to me that when children were having difficulty keeping up in kindergarten we had to put them aside and carefully watch for signs of blooming before we could teach them to read.

I am thrilled to be writing a foreword for Susan Hall's book for principals. This straightforward guide to implementing RTI is a little late for me to use with Matthew, Erica, and John. However, the timing is perfect for practitioners who are seeking research-based ways to make the gift of reading available to all students, not just to those who are "ready." I am passionate about raising reading achievement at any grade level but also realistic enough to recognize that every primary grade in which a child does not attain crucial reading benchmarks translates into 2–3 years of catch-up time in middle and high school. This is a book about giving the gift of reading to more than 95% of your students. In the meantime, reading achievement in your school and district will go up every year thereafter.

As Hall is quick to point out, RTI is not a special education initiative but an approach to revolutionizing reading instruction in your school or district. Students who are successful in acquiring grade-appropriate reading skills in the primary grades will enter third and fourth grade prepared to read to learn. They will no longer have to struggle with learning to read for years on end, potentially giving up in desperation and eventually dropping out of school.

There will be educators who resist RTI. Even though we know all we need to know to prevent reading failure in all but a very small percentage of students, it's how we feel about the fact that we haven't done it thus far that matters most. Some educators feel guilty and find it hard to admit failing the children who have passed through their classrooms. Others are fearful that they will not be able to teach them all to read. But it's time for principals and teachers in every school to forget the past, confess their fears, and then roll up their sleeves and begin to teach them all to read. I can speak from experience: There is nothing more invigorating and inspiring than to see a student who was deemed developmentally delayed or a late bloomer unlock the code and begin to read independently.

Will your teachers be challenged? Of course! Will some of them resist? Inevitably. But whose school is it? You will find all the nuts and bolts of RTI in the pages ahead. Hall provides a fascinating case study so you can see RTI in action and then takes your hand and leads you through implementation step by step. If you know almost nothing about RTI, this book provides a superb orientation. If you know a little about RTI, you will be an expert by the time you finish the book.

Preface

WHAT THIS BOOK IS ABOUT

This book is a principal's guide about how to implement Response to Intervention (RTI) to improve student reading outcomes in elementary and middle schools. RTI is a set of processes for organizing decision making for data-driven instructional practices. It is an approach whereby schools intervene first and refer students to special education only after multiple tiers of intensive help are provided and the student has responded insufficiently to intervention instruction. In addition to a set of processes and practices that are embedded in the daily life in a school, it is a paradigm, or way of thinking, about how to help students achieve reading success.

RTI can apply to other subjects and grade levels. The term describes an approach to using data to analyze how a student responds when an intervention is provided. This book focuses on the use of RTI in reading in kindergarten through middle school, with a special focus on kindergarten through third grade. Although RTI can be applied to math difficulties or high school reading difficulties, the amount and quality of research in the field of early reading provide a unique opportunity to apply the RTI approach with foundational knowledge about effective instructional practices. The body of research about the strategies and instructional practices that are most effective provides an amazing clarity about what works in teaching students how to read.

The other reason RTI is particularly well suited to early reading is the growth in well-researched early literacy screening instruments. The process of RTI depends on the effectiveness of the assessment tool in identifying which students are at risk and which are candidates for improvements through intervention instruction. Similarly, the process depends on periodically administering alternative forms of the screening instrument to determine whether the intervention instruction is helping. In early reading, these assessments are readily available and are efficient and effective.

PURPOSE OF THIS BOOK

I have dedicated more than 10 years of my career to helping schools, districts, and state departments of education implement early identification and intervention practices in reading. Before it was called RTI and before the Reading First initiative was launched in 2002, many researchers in the field of reading were encouraging schools to screen students and intervene early. These researchers were reporting encouraging findings that with early help, reading difficulties could be averted for many students.

Over the past several years I've observed many principals who believe RTI is the right thing to do and feel that a prevention model is intuitively appealing. What's not to like about it? The body of research about its effectiveness is indisputable. Yet many schools haven't launched an RTI initiative yet. What often stands in the way of implementation is a clear vision of what RTI looks like in practice. This book is a compilation of ideas and strategies about how to implement an early reading initiative, derived from my experiences consulting with hundreds of schools over the past 10 years. This book contains my recommendations about how to implement RTI. However, there are many ways to organize and implement and no single right way.

The focus of this book is on implementing RTI, not on convincing the reader that RTI is the right thing to do. I assume that most administrators who pick up this book are looking for information about how to do it. There are excellent publications on the research findings that support RTI, but an exhaustive publication of the research findings supporting RTI is not the purpose here.

WHO THIS BOOK IS FOR

The subtitle of the book is "A Principal's Guide" because the target audience is administrators at the building and district level. Although the book is not just for principals and is useful for an entire staff as an overview as they plan their implementation of RTI, the goal is to reach principals first because their leadership of RTI is critical. It's not a comprehensive manual on how to analyze student data and place students in groups. My previous book, *I've DIBEL'd, Now What?* includes more information on that topic.

Ten years ago, when I began trying to help schools implement early intervention initiatives, I naively believed that even if the principal wasn't committed to early intervention, helping a few good teacher leaders would be enough to get this done. Although it's not impossible to achieve success when the principal is not committed to leading this initiative, it is tough.

The most effective implementations occur in schools where the following factors are present:

- The principal is committed to systemically solving reading problems before it's too late and plays a significant leadership and participatory role.
- There is a motivation to make a change. There can be many reasons, including low test scores, loss of Title I funding, a large special education population, or the desire to implement it before the state or district requires you to do so. The closer the reason is to student needs, the easier it is to motivate teachers.
- At least one teacher has an adequate foundational knowledge about how to teach struggling readers and can advise the principal and coach the teachers. This person may already hold the position or be appointed to a new role with a title such as *reading coach, RTI coordinator,* or *RTI coach.*

There are many things that make it easier to implement. However, these three things top my list of essentials for success.

One other reason this book was written for principals is because of what happens to talented teachers and reading coaches when the principal is not on board and, desperate to help students, they inadvertently overstep their roles. One of the most difficult things to observe is a school where all the ingredients for a successful change are there except for one: The principal is not an instructional leader of this process. Without this leadership, the initiative is less likely to succeed. At this type of school there is typically a capable reading coach who is working hard and has enormous potential to help teachers, yet a few resistant teachers are derailing the initiative, and the principal is not addressing this disruptive behavior. The role of a reading coach, or peer teacher leader, is hard enough as it is.

Resistant teachers often question the validity of the assessment tool, claim that change isn't needed, deny the appropriateness of the instructional philosophy or strategies, or wonder aloud about how they will find the time to do all this work. Questioning and professional dialogue are a healthy part of any change process. However, there is a difference between appropriate professional learning and unprofessional behavior that misdirects frustration or anger at a peer. Too often when the principal doesn't handle the resistant teachers, it becomes a personalized battle between colleagues. It's the principal's role to get the resisters on board. Colleagues cannot and should not be expected to handle these problems with their peers when they don't have the supervisory authority to insist on implementation.

WHY THIS BOOK IS NEEDED

This book is different from existing publications. Whereas many books on RTI are too focused on special education and the related regulations, *Implementing Response to Intervention* takes a broader approach. There is indeed a strong relationship between RTI and special education, and with Title I as well. However, it is imperative that a principal position RTI as a general education initiative. Failure to do so makes it too easy for general education teachers to brush it off as something the special education teachers are responsible for doing.

Another difference in this book is that it provides for principals more practical tips about how to get started. This book provides advice on how to implement RTI in stages and what to tackle in the first year. It includes information about how to use data in meetings and how to design a year-long professional development plan to get your staff accustomed to using data to inform instructional decisions.

OVERVIEW

The scope of this book is about getting RTI launched in a school, with a particular emphasis on the first year. The book opens with a fictionalized case study of Lincoln Elementary School, which has already implemented RTI. Studying Lincoln Elementary's implementation provides a robust picture of the process in action and sets the context for the applied chapters that follow.

Chapter 1, "Why Implement RTI?" describes the forces that have led RTI to emerge so powerfully in reading. It includes background information on the inclusion of RTI in the reauthorization of the Individuals with Disability Education Act and the relationship of RTI to other reading initiatives and services such as Reading First and special education.

Chapter 2, "Setting the Stage for RTI," is helpful for planning your school's implementation. The chapter begins with what principals need to do before launching RTI. This includes ways to motivate your staff to want to implement this initiative and ideas for your communication plan. Advice is included about how to implement in stages and limit what you take on the first year. Also, important information is provided about designing your assessment plan so that you are ready with an assessment calendar, a data management system, and a plan about who will give the assessments.

Chapter 3, "Delivering Intervention Instruction," is about establishing your school's delivery system to offer tiers of instruction to meet the needs of all students. There are a variety of ways to organize groups, and models are provided. Information is included about who teaches the groups, when it happens, and where intervention groups meet. Alternative processes are presented for making decisions to move students into groups and between groups.

Chapter 4, "Using Progress Monitoring Data," contains information about why progress monitoring is an integral part of RTI, how to determine which skills to monitor, and how to graph a student's rate of progress. Also covered in this chapter is how RTI schools use data in many types of meetings, including grade-level team meetings, principal meetings with individual teachers, and meetings with parents.

Chapter 5, "Effective Models of Professional Development," outlines how to design a professional development plan to get RTI started. A description of a sustained, job-embedded professional development model is included. A professional development plan should include workshops, grade-level meetings, and one-on-one coaching and conferencing with teachers. A plan is explored that includes providing professional development in strands for administrators, RTI coordinators and reading coaches, and teachers.

Chapter 6, "What the Future Holds for RTI," examines the implications of RTI today and how it may affect upper grade levels and other curricula in the coming years.

Acknowledgments

I would like to acknowledge many people who have allowed me to learn along with them. There are so many teachers, principals, and district administrators who have given me the opportunity to work beside them. Thank you to James Baker, Dreama Bell, Glennie Buckley, Sue Cartwright, Jeanne Corbin, Tina Erwin, Marge Fostiak, Chris Grode, Judith Guild, Barbara Kurth, Teena Linch, Debbie Lyon, Linda Nolan, Linda Palenchar, Dennis Pauli, Linda Proehl, Ethel Sacha, Mary Tracey, Deb Warner, Susan Wilson, and Debbie Wood.

Thanks to the consultants of 95 Percent Group, who are willing to come along on this journey and learn with me. I respect their knowledge and insights as we continue to improve our work with schools.

I would like to express my appreciation for my relationship with Louisa Moats. She has taught me about the English language in ways that have forever changed what I have to offer to teachers today. The knowledge she has given me as a Language Essentials for Teachers of Reading and Spelling (LETRS) trainer and coauthor and the support she offers me as a friend empower me to continue traveling weekly to reach out to as many teachers as I can.

Corwin Press gratefully acknowledges the contributions of the following people:

Jennifer Cruz
Principal
Mirage Elementary School
Glendale, AZ

Tonya Middling
Coordinator, Learning Improvement
Office of Superintendent of Public Instruction, Special Education
Olympia, WA

Alice Hom
Principal
Yung Wing Elementary
New York, NY

Patti Kinney
Principal
Talent Middle School
Talent, OR

About the Author

 **Susan L. Hall**, EdD, is a consultant specializing in teacher training in reading. She is founder and president of an education consulting and professional development company called 95 Percent Group Inc. The company provides consulting and teacher training to districts and schools in how to use early literacy screening data from the Dynamic Indicators of Basic Early Literacy Skills (DIBELS) assessment to inform data-driven small-group tiers of intervention to address specific skill deficits. Susan is a nationally certified trainer of DIBELS and LETRS. She served as a consultant to several state departments of education in the implementation of professional development associated with the Reading First program and with RTI initiatives. Susan is coauthor with Louisa Moats of two books, *Straight Talk About Reading* and *Parenting a Struggling Reader*, and author of a best-selling book called *I've DIBEL'd, Now What?*

It is not uncommon for clients of 95 Percent Group to dramatically improve their school's reading scores, even in the first year of working with the company. With aggressive implementation of RTI procedures, many schools increase their DIBELS scores from less than 40% of kindergartners at benchmark at the beginning of the year to 95% at the end of the first year. Often first-grade results exceed 90% in year one, and second grade and above can exceed 90% with a couple of years of implementation. The company provides a long-term, sustained form of professional development on RTI with meetings with principals, teacher workshops, grade-level teacher meetings, and follow-up visits to coach teachers in how to intensify intervention instruction.

If you have questions or need a sounding board as you work through the implementation phases, contact me at shall@95percentgroup.com or through my consulting firm at

95 Percent Group Inc.
1477 Barclay Blvd.
Buffalo Grove, IL 60089
(847) 499-8200

LINCOLN ELEMENTARY SCHOOL

A Case Study of What RTI Looks Like in a School

In 31 years of working with students, this is the most important work I've ever done.

—Intervention teacher

One of the best ways to see what RTI looks like in a school is to visit a school that has increased student reading scores as a result of implementing RTI processes and practices. In this case study we will do exactly that. The description that follows is of a fictitious school named Lincoln Elementary School, whose principal will be called Ms. Smith.

EVIDENCE OF BUY-IN

As you visit Lincoln Elementary School, one of the things you notice is that the staff embraces a paradigm of early intervention. There is a strong belief that RTI helps teachers help struggling readers. The staff knows that RTI is about prevention of reading problems, and the best way to prevent problems is to intervene as early as possible. Because reading trajectories are established early, it's imperative to get all students reading well by the end of first grade and keep them there. It's easier to deliver good first teaching during the language arts block, and proactive early intervention in kindergarten through third grade, than to remediate in fourth grade and beyond. Getting a slow start increases a student's odds of failure. In this school it is viewed as too risky to conclude that a below-benchmark student is simply experiencing a developmental lag that he or she will outgrow. The staff explains to visitors that all below-benchmark students receive intervention because it's better to intervene unnecessarily than to postpone intervention and lose valuable months when intervention is most effective. Because the school administers progress monitoring assessments regularly, teachers can exit a student if he or she catches up quickly.

> *It's easier to deliver good first teaching during the language arts block, and proactive early intervention in kindergarten through third grade, than to remediate in fourth grade and beyond.*

When you ask the Lincoln staff whether there is any research behind RTI, they have answers. They tell you that students leaving first grade behind in reading are likely to remain behind their peers. They know that providing intervention earlier is more efficient and possibly even more effective. One teacher pipes up to explain that, according to research, it takes four times as long to intervene in fourth grade as in kindergarten. Some students who receive help too late never develop the level of fluency of those who get help earlier. Teachers know that, according to intervention research studies, less than 5% of students fail to meet benchmark when effective RTI practices are in place in a school. Lincoln School's staff is motivated to reach the goal of 95% of students reading on grade level. You have to wonder whether it's Ms. Smith's leadership or the staff's strong knowledge about RTI that explains their encouraging attitude. There is a no-excuses belief that their students can read if the staff can just figure out what instructional approach is needed. Not once will you hear a teacher say that a student can't read because there's no support at home.

The teachers at Lincoln School are persistent in their approach to trying different intervention instructional strategies until the right solution is found. Along with that relentless tweaking of instruction is a commitment that all students not at benchmark are entitled to small-group intervention. Have you ever visited a school where the intervention services were focused on students just slightly below benchmark in the high-stakes testing grade level? What you find is that the staff is uncomfortable because they know that this approach is an attempt to boost the school's test scores and artificially inflate the position of the school at the expense of the students. At Lincoln School the mission is to provide intervention to *all* children whose scores are below benchmark, with a focus on the early years, not the high-stakes testing grades.

In addition to entitlement and a relentless persistence for results, one of the most profound observations is that the lines between staff roles have blurred. The special education teachers are working side by side with the general education classroom teachers rather than in resource rooms, sometimes helping children with radically different needs. Special education teachers provide focused instruction to small groups in the general education classrooms during intervention block times. Title I and English-language learner (ELL) teachers are included in data meetings with classroom teachers. Those who work with struggling readers are making collaborative decisions. Ms. Smith saw RTI as a golden opportunity to finally align the staff and break down the departmental walls between special education, general education, Title I, and ELL staff.

The attitudes described here are intangible. However, some procedures and practices in an RTI school can be observed directly. Three times a year there is a flurry of activity as the staff completes universal screening of all students in the building (K–5). Lincoln School uses an early literacy screening assessment called the Dynamic Indicators of Basic Early Literacy Skills (DIBELS). Another observable set of activities is the procedures teachers use to make data-driven decisions about students. During grade-level team meetings and individual planning sessions, teachers place students in groups to receive alternative tiers of instruction to meet their needs.

The delivery model for reading instruction is especially well organized in Lincoln School. Rather than a one-size-fits-all approach, teachers have a menu of options for what may work best for an individual student. Every student (or nearly every student) participates in what is called the core instruction, otherwise known as Tier I. Students who do not reach benchmark with Tier I instruction alone are placed in the first line of intervention, which adds extra time for reading instruction in Tier II. The Tier II groups meet daily for 30 minutes of intervention, with no more than five students in a group. If the student still is making inadequate progress after a reasonable period of time and after adjustments to intensify instruction, he or she is moved from the Tier II small group to a Tier III group that meets for an hour and has no more than three students.

The curriculum materials used in each of the tiers are as diverse as the allocations of intervention instruction time and the size of the groups. Lincoln School purchased a core reading curriculum and trained teachers in the instructional strategies embedded in the program so that Tier I instruction is fairly uniform between classrooms. In order to provide materials for Tier II, the staff selected a handful of programs from the more than 200 commercially available intervention programs. Teachers chose which materials to use for each intervention group based on the focus of instruction for the group. Some groups receive instruction using materials from a program for phonics intervention, another for fluency intervention, and still other groups use materials from a vocabulary and oral language program. Teachers have access to book rooms with different types of texts and skill bags that contain prepared materials to check out for the week to help them teach small group lessons on phonological awareness and phonics skills. Lincoln School also purchased a Tier III program with a curriculum that is even more systematic, explicit, and sequential than that of Tier II, with slower pacing and more repetition cycles than the core program.

ASSESSMENT PROCEDURES

Because Lincoln School is in the middle of its second year of implementing RTI, the procedures for collecting and managing data are well established. The school is committed to universal screening of all students, and therefore they have instituted screening procedures. The staff knows when assessments are administered, who assesses which students, and what happens with the data.

The spring before implementation, Ms. Smith sent five staff members to a workshop on administering and scoring the DIBELS. This assessment team collected baseline data on all the students in May before launching into RTI the following September. Although these five assessment team members tested all the students at the beginning, that pilot period lasted only a short time. The principal decided that because the purpose of the RTI assessment data is to inform decisions about instruction, it was essential that teachers administer the assessments and observe how their students perform. Just before school started in year one of RTI, the entire staff attended a workshop on administration and scoring of DIBELS.

> The principal decided that because the purpose of the RTI assessment data is to inform decisions about instruction, it was essential that teachers administer the assessments and observe how their students perform.

The procedures implemented at Lincoln School were instrumental in their rapidly becoming proficient at administering the assessments and gathering high-quality data. During the fall benchmark in year one, teachers were paired up so that one assessor gave the student the directions and wrote his or her answers in the student scoring booklet while another teacher shadow scored. The second staff member, the one who shadow scored, listened and also recorded the student's answers on a duplicate copy of the probes. After the student walked away, the two assessors compared their scoring pages and consulted the RTI coordinator when they were unsure about any scoring procedures. This shadow scoring procedure is still used when a new staff member joins the school.

A couple of other processes help ensure high-quality data. The week before the three benchmark assessments, the RTI coordinator attends each grade-level team meeting to review the scoring procedures for the upcoming assessment. Because the indicators are different across the year at some grade levels, a refresher is useful. Another procedure to ensure high-quality screening data is a random retest. The week after benchmark testing, assessment team members pull a sample of 10% of the students in each class to retest with a progress monitoring probe to ensure that the original and retest scores are reasonably close. Because some teachers give the assessments infrequently, the random retest catches any scoring mistakes. It is possible to retest if needed. Because the benchmark data are critical in determining which students need intervention, the data must be of high quality.

Lincoln School has a published assessment calendar. The fall, winter, and spring benchmark assessments are all completed within a 2-week period, and the calendar designates every third week for progress monitoring. The school's academic year has three benchmark periods and eight progress monitoring periods. Some students are progress monitored weekly, as determined by their participation in a Tier III group or the teacher's concern.

Although in some schools the student scoring booklets are collected and filed, in this school teachers are committed to using the data. Therefore, the teachers keep the student scoring booklets in their classrooms, and the school provides plastic filing boxes with handles so the teachers can carry all their scoring booklets to data meetings. After a benchmark and progress monitoring period, each teacher enters his or her class data into a simple Excel spreadsheet and e-mails the class scores to the RTI coordinator, who then inputs the data into the University of Oregon's data management system. Once the data are in the database, the RTI coordinator prints reports to update the data notebooks for the principal and herself. Teachers go online to print their own reports.

Ms. Smith is so committed to ensuring that the staff uses the data that in the first year of RTI implementation, the school contracted for outside consulting and professional development. She had learned from visiting other schools that a major impediment to full implementation of RTI occurs when teachers have the data but don't know how to analyze them. Early elementary teachers are accustomed to using data to assess whether students learned the content of a unit taught, but they need help in learning how to use formative data to make instructional decisions. The professional development was job embedded and sustained across the first year of implementation. The teachers attended an initial workshop by grade levels to learn techniques for analyzing the data to determine skill deficits, placing students in small groups, and planning intervention instruction. Several times during year one, the school's RTI consultant came back for follow-up. The consultant facilitated grade-level meetings to help teachers dig deeper in the data to form focus groups and lesson planning for intervention groups, to analyze progress monitoring data, and to use techniques to intensify instruction for the students making insufficient progress. The consultant also observed students in intervention groups and met teachers one on one to provide feedback and assistance. The consulting included year-long mentoring and problem solving for the RTI coordinator and principal.

> She had learned from visiting other schools that a major impediment to full implementation of RTI occurs when teachers have the data but don't know how to analyze them.

> However, belief and commitment alone will not create change. It is the presence of key processes that defines an RTI school. Perhaps even more important than screening are the processes for using data to make decisions about students.

Teachers at Lincoln School have embraced the use of data to inform decisions. However, belief and commitment alone will not create change. It is the presence of key processes that defines an RTI school. Perhaps even more important than screening are the processes for using data to make decisions about students. At Lincoln School, after each benchmark assessment, the data are used initially to make decisions about placement of below-benchmark students into small groups to receive intervention instruction. The staff determines an instructional focus for each group and decides whether the group is a Tier II or a Tier III group, based on their needs. The materials and amount of time the group meets are then determined. A schedule is constructed based on who will teach each group. Within 1 week after the benchmark data are collected, all the groups are formed and begin meeting right away; no time is lost.

Scheduling intervention groups is one of the most challenging parts of this process. Luckily, Ms. Smith did her research as she was thinking about launching RTI at Lincoln School. While attending a workshop, Ms. Smith met a principal from a school in a neighboring district whose RTI implementation was about a year ahead. When Ms. Smith visited the school, their principal emphasized how critical it is to have key staff members involved in creating a schedule that will work for all stakeholders.

TIERS OF INSTRUCTION

Tier I

Lincoln School has a designated time in the school day for the 90-minute English Language Arts (ELA) block. The master schedule has the 90-minute ELA block for first grade occurring from 9:00 to 10:30 daily. A wide variety of grouping structures are used during the block, including time for instruction as a whole class and in small groups and time for students to work independently in literacy work stations (sometimes called centers).

Although schools may use a wide variety of curricula, including teacher-designed materials, Lincoln School uses a published reading program. Because of declining reading scores and the complexity of teaching reading, 2 years ago the adoption committee recommended the purchase of a published program to provide teachers with a curriculum for Tier I. Some teachers call it a basal program. Throughout the classrooms the materials are in use, including the teacher's guides, student books, and many other supplemental materials such as CD-ROMs, puppets, and letter cards.

As you walk in and out of first-grade classrooms at Lincoln School, all the teachers are teaching lessons from the same week within their program. Although there are differences between the classes, one benefit of having a published program is that the teachers collaborate extensively in lesson preparation and benefit from the prepared materials that the program provides. Because students may receive intervention instruction from someone other than their classroom teacher, it is important that consistent techniques and cueing systems are used for critical strategies such as learning to blend sounds to read words.

The school's student population has changed dramatically over the past 5 years, and some of their former approaches to teaching reading aren't as effective with the more diverse student population. They carefully studied the reasons for the gradual decline in their scores, so when they adopted a published core program, it was with a great deal of thought and research.

> Because students may receive intervention instruction from someone other than their classroom teacher, it is important that consistent techniques and cueing systems are used for critical strategies such as learning to blend sounds to read words.

Their efforts to improve reading instruction have paid off, and Lincoln School is making gains; however, they are still below the recommended goal of 70%–80% of students reaching benchmark with Tier I instruction alone (Vaughn Gross Center for Reading and Language Arts, 2005, p. 12).

Tier II

After the conclusion of the Tier I ELA block at Lincoln, all first-grade classes provide Tier II small-group time from 10:30 to 11:00. This instruction generally is the first layer of small-group instruction provided for students not at benchmark. Interventions are *not* preferential seating, shortened assignments, or lowered expectations; these can be considered accommodations instead of interventions. The instruction provided in Tier II is focused on addressing the core deficit skills rather than teaching strategies to cope with gaps.

In first grade, intervention is delivered in the homeroom classroom. As you enter the classroom during the intervention block you will see the teacher at a horseshoe-shaped table in one corner with her back to the wall and her eyes observing the rest of the classroom. Positioning the students with their backs to the classroom helps reduce their temptation to watch students working nearby at independent work stations. The teacher is teaching one intervention group of five below-benchmark students while a Title I teacher is at another table with a group of three of the lowest-performing students. These students were selected for placement in homogeneous groups so that all the students are deficient in a specific skill area. Lincoln School believes that heterogeneous grouping is important for much of reading instruction; however, during intervention group time, the groups must be homogeneous by skill deficit. Because the groups are formed in this way, the instruction can be focused on a specific area. Teachers are quick to remind visitors that these are skill groups, not ability groups.

The classroom teacher's group is working on a phonics lesson in early alphabetic principle. It is late January, and she has grouped together five students who did not reach benchmark on the Oral Reading Fluency (ORF) or Nonsense Word Fluency (NWF) indicator in DIBELS. After seeing the low scores on reading passages in the ORF of the DIBELS and analyzing the pattern of errors made in the NWF indicator, the teacher decided she wanted more diagnostic data on exactly what types of word patterns these students can and cannot read. DIBELS tells who needs intervention but doesn't always provide enough information about what type of instruction they need. To dig deeper and get a more diagnostic view, the teachers at Lincoln School use an informal assessment known as the Phonics Screener for Intervention™ (95 Percent Group Inc., 2006).

> DIBELS tells who needs intervention but doesn't always provide enough information about what type of instruction they need.

The data from the phonics screener show which type of words each struggling reader in the class is unable to read. The five students in this group were placed together because all are unable to pass Skills 2, 3, or 4 on the phonics screener, which measures the ability to read consonant–vowel–consonant words (CVC), words with short vowels and consonant blends (e.g., *stop, jump*), and digraphs (e.g., *ship, wish, chip*). These concepts were taught in October through December in the core program, yet assessment verified that these students had not mastered the ability to read words with these patterns. By working with these students in a small group, the teacher hopes to provide explicit instruction, adequate corrective feedback, and opportunities for sufficient practice with scaffolding to enable the students to master the concepts. She knows that these students will need an explicit lesson using the modeling structure of "I do, we do, and you do." The students can begin by watching the teacher model how to read words with these patterns. Then, because she has only five students, she can observe each one closely and provide immediate corrections when they make errors.

The teacher has prepared a lesson plan for her group with a very structured lesson. There are six components of this phonics lesson plan: review, teach new concept, read words, build words, sentence dictation, and transfer to text. The first component is a very short review of a previously taught concept, lasting about 3 minutes. She asks the students to read about 30 words as she flips word cards. The entire group reads the first 10 words, and then she asks them to take turns on the next 20 words, with each child reading one word during each of the five rounds. All these words had the "short *a*" pattern, which was last week's target skill.

The second component of the lesson is to teach the new skill this week, which is instruction on "short *i*" words. The teacher starts the lesson by asking the students to respond with "thumbs up" when they hear a short /i/ sound in the middle of pronounced words or "thumbs down" for words with short /a/ sound. After it is clear that all the students can hear the difference in these two short vowel sounds, she writes the letter *i* on the whiteboard behind her and states that this is the letter used to spell the sound /i/, as in the word *itch.* She demonstrates a gesture of holding out a forearm and scratching an itch while saying the sound "/i/" multiple times.

The lesson continues when the teacher states that the objective of today's lesson is learning to read words with the short /i/ sound. She asks the students to watch her. After writing the word *it* on her whiteboard she points to the letter *i* and says "/i/," points to the letter *t* and says "/t/," and finally scoops her finger under the word and says "it." She says, "Watch me," and models again. After modeling the "I do," she then writes another word and asks the students to join her in reading the words for the "we do" portion of the lesson. They read the word *sit* together. Then they read the word *pit* together. She points to one word at a time and asks a student to read it. After it is clear that all students can read these words, she moves to the "you do" portion of the lesson. She hands each student an index card with a list of about eight words. After telling them that each of their lists contains different words, they read their cards quietly as she listens to each student read words, providing feedback where necessary.

The third and fourth components of the lesson are word reading and word building. The teacher models reading words and sorting word cards in columns based on the middle vowel sounds. They practice a few words together (the "we do" part), and then she hands each student a deck of cards to read and sort. The teacher starts the word building component of the lesson plan by modeling spelling words with a pocket chart that contains six consonant letters and the two vowels *a* and *i.* The teacher moves letter cards for a consonant *s,* vowel *i,* and consonant *t* from the top pocket down to the bottom pocket. She reads the word *sit* while scooping her finger under the word. Then she says, "If this says *sit,* watch me make it say *pit.*" This instruction is systematic in that the teacher follows the same cueing system when she asks them to spell words later. Next she hands each student a pocket chart with the same letters, and she dictates words for the students to spell, one at a time, until they have practiced writing 10 different words, all containing the "short *i*" pattern. The teacher has learned that although this level of explicitness is not necessary for her benchmark students, it has been effective in helping with her struggling students.

The fifth component of the lesson is sentence dictation. The teacher dictates two sentences, and the students write them. The sentences are "The big rig is in the pit" and "Tim hit the bat." After the students write each sentence on their paper, the teacher writes them on the whiteboard behind her, and they correct their work.

The sixth and final component of the lesson plan is to transfer skills from reading at the word level to reading passages. The teacher hands each student a copy of a three-paragraph decodable passage. *Decodable* means that it contains word patterns that the student has previously mastered and so should be able to read without guessing. The passage selected has many examples of words with the "short *i*" pattern, so the students are able to practice reading words with the target pattern. First, students find the "short *i*" words and highlight them. Then they chorally read the highlighted words aloud. Finally, the teacher asks the students to use their phonics phones (a curved piece of plastic pipe) so they can hear themselves whisper reading the story while the teacher listens to one student at a time read it aloud to her. This structured phonics lesson plan was completed in 30 minutes.

Tier III

Tier III is an even more intensive layer of instruction available for students who did not reach benchmark after receiving instruction for a reasonable amount of time in Tiers I and II. What qualifies as a "reasonable" period of time varies, but at Lincoln School teachers typically provide at least one round of 8–10 weeks in Tier II before recommending consideration for Tier III. All but a handful of students who are moved directly to Tier III have completed multiple rounds of Tier II. Instruction is intensified during the multiple rounds of Tier II by placement in a smaller group or one where different instructional strategies are used. As concern increases about insufficient progress, the teacher keeps a more detailed intervention log, sometimes noting how many times a concept was taught and not mastered. Often a copy of the lesson plan for the week is attached to the intervention log to demonstrate evidence of the degree of explicitness and systematic nature of the instruction provided.

As is the case in most schools, at Lincoln School Tier III is still not special education. Lack of sufficient progress is perhaps the most highly trusted indicator in the discussion about whether to refer a student for testing for special education qualification. In this school the number of referrals for evaluation for special education services has dropped precipitously, yet the students referred are younger, and nearly always the referred student is qualified. Ms. Smith has commented that teachers speak with much more conviction about referrals now because they have solid assessment and observation data to know what instruction the child has received.

> *Lack of sufficient progress is perhaps the most highly trusted indicator in the discussion about whether to refer a student for testing for special education qualification.*

The instruction in Tier III is more intensive and is scheduled at a time that is outside the Tier I reading block and for more time than Tier II. For many Tier III groups, the staff at Lincoln School uses a program that is more intensive, with systematic and sequential instruction and built-in review and repetition. Often this is scheduled for two 30-minute blocks or one 60-minute block.

The assessment in Tier III is also more intensive, with weekly progress monitoring. Weekly assessments help teachers carefully examine rates of progress, and trend lines are more reliable because there are more data points.

DATA-DRIVEN DECISION MAKING

Data Discussions at Grade-Level Meetings

Although Ms. Smith doesn't attend all weekly grade-level meetings, she is present at least monthly to evaluate student progress and learn of any issues to resolve. At the first meeting of each month, the RTI coordinator prepares an update on the current progress of the students at the grade level. The chart displays the percentage of students at the three instructional recommendation levels: benchmark, strategic, and intensive. These data are available on several reports in the DIBELS data system. Lincoln School prefers to take these data from a report and create a graph by using a simple spreadsheet in Excel (see Figure A).

Figure A   Lincoln School DIBELS Scores for Grades K–3

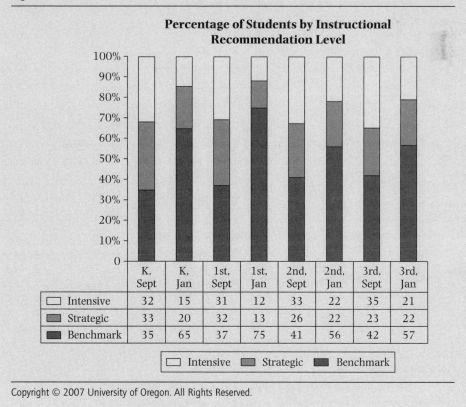

	K, Sept	K, Jan	1st, Sept	1st, Jan	2nd, Sept	2nd, Jan	3rd, Sept	3rd, Jan
☐ Intensive	32	15	31	12	33	22	35	21
▥ Strategic	33	20	32	13	26	22	23	22
▰ Benchmark	35	65	37	75	41	56	42	57

☐ Intensive   ▥ Strategic   ▰ Benchmark

In addition to exploring the current reading scores, it's helpful to discuss how much progress has been made from the beginning of the year to the current time.

Today the principal attends the first-grade team meeting because the midyear benchmark assessment data have just been completed. The first chart the RTI coordinator displays shows how well the students in the school are doing. With 75% of first-grade students at benchmark, 13% at strategic, and 12% at intensive, the team celebrates. The team then looks at a second graph, which compares student progress from last year to this year (Table A). The students entered first grade stronger in some skills this year than last year because of the extensive interventions taught in kindergarten, but the substantial progress for the first half of first grade is evident.

Table A Lincoln School Grade 1 DIBELS Scores Comparison of This Year With Last Year

| | Fall | | Winter | | |
	Last Year	This Year	Last Year	This Year	Goal
Benchmark	35%	55%	50%	75%	90%
Strategic	40%	25%	30%	13%	6%
Intensive	25%	20%	20%	12%	4%

The grade-level team uses a data wall that is mounted on a whiteboard and is placed in a closet between meetings. Each student's scores are recorded on a card with a magnet glued to the back. The cards are color coded for the instructional recommendation level to which the student was assigned by the DIBELS data management system at the beginning of the year. The cards are laminated, so the student's scores are written with an erasable marker and updated as new data become available. Each card is placed on the whiteboard in one of three areas depending on the student's current instructional recommendation level. All students who are at benchmark are in the category at the top third of the board above a green line. Students currently at the strategic level are placed in the middle of the board between the green and yellow horizontal lines, and the students whose scores indicate they are intensive are at the bottom third of the board between the yellow and red lines. This data wall gives a quick view of how many students are at each instructional recommendation level. Because the cards are color coded by the student's level at the beginning of the year, the data wall shows a quick count of how many students have moved up one and two levels since the beginning of the year. On Lincoln's first-grade board only one student fell from strategic down to intensive, which the staff calls slippage.

> Because the cards are color coded by the student's level at the beginning of the year, the data wall shows a quick count of how many students have moved up one and two levels since the beginning of the year.

Goal Setting

Ms. Smith raises a question about whether the teachers still believe that the year-end goal of 90% of students at benchmark is achievable; the grade-level team set that goal in early October and has been measuring progress against that goal since then. One teacher, a veteran who initially resisted RTI, speaks up right away. She comments that although she was a bit reluctant about this initiative originally, she has seen amazing progress since the school implemented RTI. She says that the difference is evident not only because students are entering first grade with much stronger skills than ever before but also because she can see the progress struggling readers are making since they started the intervention groups and have been consistently tracking progress with data. She glances at the data wall and says that the year-end goal of 90% is very achievable, given where the students are at this point in early February.

The discussion continues, with more teachers chiming in to reflect about how much less time was spent this fall on instructing the students in phonemic awareness than in prior years. Because the students came into first grade with more skills in manipulating sounds in words, the focus of instruction could be placed on alphabetic principle, enabling students to become proficient at reading CVC word patterns by December. Now that it is early February, the focus is on fluent blending rather than accuracy while reading simple passages. Although a few students are still struggling with CVC words, they are far fewer than ever before at this time of year. A second teacher speaks up about how she is able to use more of the books in her room than in the past few years. She comments that her students' spelling is better, not just their reading.

The principal then asks whether teachers have examined the data of the students who are at benchmark in order to avoid any potential slippage. One teacher speaks up and mentions that she has completed error pattern analysis worksheets on all her students who have reached benchmark but at an accuracy level below 95% of words read correctly. Two types of errors are evident from that analysis:

- Acquisition of nonphonetic sight words was too slow.
- Students were confused about words with short vowels as they were learning the long vowel–silent *e* pattern.

Ms. Smith asks all teachers to analyze their data before the next team meeting to see how many benchmark students are at risk of slippage by year-end if not addressed.

The entire team discusses strategies to help with the two issues raised. One teacher shares that she has assessed her students with the Dolch sight word list. She has created individual rings of sight words so students can practice the words they don't know. She has noticed that some students have attached them to their belt loops and review their words while waiting in line at the drinking fountain. This teacher offers to provide the other teachers with a copy of the materials she has created.

Then the teachers turn their attention to discussing how to address the long and short vowel confusions. One teacher says that she likes using the skill bags for this because they have word cards for sorts. The RTI coordinator steps out to get some sample skill bags from the book room and returns with them so the teachers can spread the materials out on the table and share ways they have used these materials in their instruction on vowels.

Data Discussions at One-on-One Teacher Meetings

Principals can show the importance of RTI data by using data when meeting individually with teachers. One of the most useful types of graphs for such meetings is shown in Figure B. This graph shows the progress of each student from the beginning of the year to the current period. It is helpful to see how much improvement each student has made.

Figure B   Sample Line Graph of Progress by Student

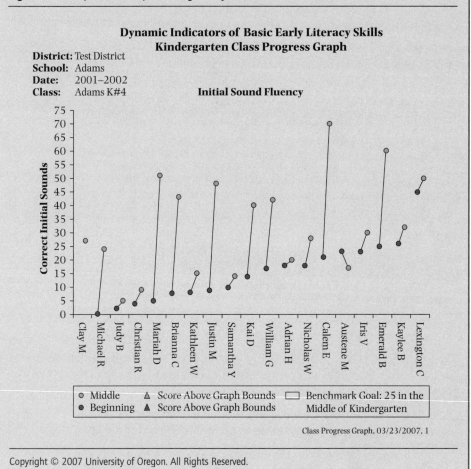

Dynamic Indicators of Basic Early Literacy Skills
Kindergarten Class Progress Graph

District: Test District
School: Adams
Date: 2001–2002
Class: Adams K#4

Initial Sound Fluency

Class Progress Graph, 03/23/2007, 1

A neighboring school that has implemented RTI developed a process that combines the grade-level and one-on-one teacher meetings in a unique manner. Every Friday afternoon there are data meetings attended by the RTI coordinator, Title I coordinator, special education teacher, and principal. The RTI coordinator's schedule on Friday afternoon is cleared of student group meetings so that she can spend time reviewing progress monitoring data and helping teachers plan for the next week's interventions. Teachers come in one at a time to discuss students who are not making sufficient progress. The conversation generally starts with the progress monitoring data confirming an insufficient rate of progress and continues with a discussion about what intervention has been provided so far. The conversation continues with a deeper look into the error patterns in the student probes. Afterward, the team may decide to collect more diagnostic data to make sure that there is laser clarity about the student's deficit skill areas before deciding what changes to make in his or her instruction. Because all staff serving that student are in the meeting, it is a very collaborative process. Decisions are made about moving students up to a higher group, back to a group working on a lower skill, or to a group that meets for twice as many minutes per week.

> *The conversation continues with a deeper look into the error patterns in the student probes, after which the team may decide to collect more diagnostic data to make sure that there is laser clarity about the student's deficit skill areas before deciding what changes to make to his or her instruction.*

Data Discussions at Parent Conferences

At Lincoln School, teachers have just begun experimenting with discussing assessment data at parent conferences, where appropriate. One consistent observation is that the data are particularly helpful when teachers need to show a parent the size of a gap between the student's current level of performance and the benchmark level. Teachers prefer using a graph to show this gap (Figure C). By seeing a trend line from at least three progress monitoring points to the end of the year, parents can see whether the student will reach benchmark in the future if his or her skills continue to respond to the instruction at the same pace as in the past.

Teachers have commented to Ms. Smith that when they show a parent the progress monitoring graph with scores plotted for periodic assessments, parents develop more confidence that the school is closely watching their child's reading. This progress monitoring chart can serve as a springboard for a conversation about what activities the parent can do at home to support the school's efforts.

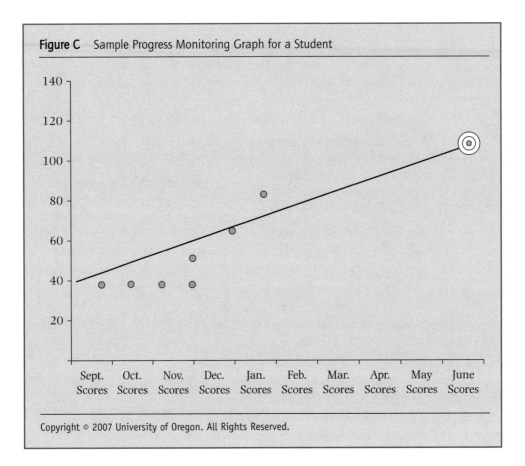

Figure C   Sample Progress Monitoring Graph for a Student

Why Implement RTI?

One of the great things is the collaboration between staff—the way we work together for the benefit of children.

—Kindergarten teacher

WHAT IS RESPONSE TO INTERVENTION?

According to the National Association of State Directors of Special Education (NASDSE), Response to Intervention (RTI) "is a practice of providing high-quality instruction and interventions matched to student need, monitoring progress frequently to make decisions about changes in instruction or goals and applying child response data to important educational decisions" (NASDSE, 2006, p. 3). The RTI process is a collaborative effort whereby educators in a school or school system jointly take responsibility to help all students learn to read. RTI is not a program or a method for teaching reading. It is a dynamic problem-solving process in which data are integral in making decisions about what skills struggling readers lack and whether intervention instruction provided to date has been effective. Although RTI can apply to math and other subjects, it's become most popular for reading instruction in the early elementary years.

> *Response to Intervention is a dynamic problem-solving process in which data are integral in making decisions about what skills struggling readers lack, and whether intervention instruction provided to date has been effective.*

Implementation of RTI in a school revolves around a deep understanding and commitment to a set of beliefs about students and early reading. Four of these fundamental beliefs are as follows:

- Preventive action is better than the wait-to-fail approach.
- Early intervention is more effective than later remediation.
- Universal screening helps prevent students from falling through the cracks.
- Tiers of instruction are available to meet the needs of all students.

These ideas are part of the belief system of schools that have successfully implemented RTI.

The role of RTI is much broader than simply a procedure to determine whether a student qualifies for special education services. The title of a recent publication by the Michigan Association for Administrators of Special Education indicates a broader definition of RTI. In *Response to Intervention: Enhancing the Learning of All Children*, the organization articulates two roles of RTI:

> The narrow role is that of a gate-keeper for eligibility, e.g., it helps to establish that the child's learning problems are not due to lack of appropriate instruction, and to establish that the child's problems are posing such an adverse impact that the child needs special education in order to benefit from his/her education. The larger role is the continued application of the RTI core principles in the IEP [Individualized Education Plan] process itself: problem-solving; using scientific, research-based interventions; monitoring student progress; and using assessment and progress data to make decisions. (Heinzelman & LaPointe, 2006, p. 7)

EIGHT CORE PRINCIPLES OF RTI

> It may look easy once in place, but getting from where your school is now to full implementation is rarely simple. Many variables affect how difficult the implementation will be, but perhaps the most important one is leadership.

One of the best resources on RTI is a publication by the NASDSE titled *Response to Intervention: Policy Considerations and Implementation* (2006). This publication lists eight core principles of RTI. These principles cover the important characteristics of what makes RTI much broader than a qualification procedure for special education (Table 1.1).

Lincoln Elementary, the RTI school described in the case study, sounds like a well-oiled machine. In many ways it is because a set of processes and procedures is in place, and the staff knows what to do and how to do it. It

Table 1.1   Eight Core Principles of Response to Intervention

I	We can effectively teach all children.
II	Intervene early.
III	Use a multi-tier model of service delivery.
IV	Use a problem-solving model to make decisions within a multi-tier model.
V	Use scientific, research-based validated intervention and instruction to the extent available.
VI	Monitor student progress to inform instruction.
VII	Use data to make decisions. A data-based decision regarding student response to intervention is central to RTI practices.
VIII	Use assessment for screening, diagnostics, and progress monitoring.

From Batsche, G. et al., in *Response to Intervention: Policy Considerations and Implementation,* Copyright © 2006, pp. 19–20. Reprinted with permission from NASDSE.

may look easy once in place, but getting from where your school is now to full implementation is rarely simple. Many variables affect how difficult the implementation will be. Perhaps the most important one is leadership. Implementing RTI is complex and challenging, and so knowing up front *why* you are leading an RTI initiative is important. If you don't believe in it, the journey is going to be very difficult.

It's hard to imagine how anyone can question RTI. It's the right thing to do for children. It's logical and makes sense. Yet some of your staff will resist, not because they don't believe in RTI principles but because RTI entails changing how time is spent, how instruction is delivered, and who works with which students. Some staff will be threatened by changes in things that are so important to them. An unfaltering commitment is essential because you will be presented with many reasons your staff doesn't want to do this. Be ready with answers that show that you've done your research and given this a great deal of thought.

This chapter provides the necessary background information so that principals can respond to questions and challenges. It includes information about the forces that drove the inclusion of RTI in federal laws. There are terms that are important to be familiar with, and it also helps to know a little about how the final version of the Individuals with Disability Education Act (IDEA) 2004 allows for RTI as a process for determining whether a student is eligible for special education services.

Many principals know a great deal about special education law and practices and will choose to skim this chapter. If you don't have a strong background in special education law, this information will help you speak with your special education staff about RTI. Special education teachers are likely to approach RTI with different terminology than teachers in general education. You will have to provide the bridge to get everyone on the same page.

SHAPING THE INITIATIVE

Reconsider the eight core principles of RTI, as identified by the NASDSE in its 2006 publication *Response to Intervention: Policy Considerations and Implementation* (see Table 1.1). These core principles must be important points in your communication plan. They are the fundamental beliefs underpinning RTI, and these principles clarify what to emphasize when discussing RTI implementation with your staff.

WHY RTI IS MORE THAN A SPECIAL EDUCATION REQUIREMENT

The NASDSE suggests a definition of RTI that is broader than merely a qualification approach for students who have reading disabilities. They define RTI as the practice of providing high-quality instruction and interventions and basing decisions on child outcome data, including progress monitoring data. NASDSE provides the following guidance in their publication *Response to Intervention: Policy Considerations and Implementation*:

> RTI should be applied to decisions in general, remedial, and special education, creating a well-integrated system of instruction/intervention guided by child outcome data. (NASDSE, 2006, p. 3)

The NASDSE publication describes an integrated special education and general education delivery model to ensure that all children are making progress, as measured by a student's level of performance and learning rate.

An RTI process may be required by your district or state for the special education qualification process, yet emphasizing this requirement as the main justification for implementing RTI may have a limiting effect. That position makes it too easy for classroom teachers to dismiss this initiative as something that special education teachers are responsible for delivering. From time to time it's helpful to tell a resistant staff member that what you're requesting is required by the government or the district office. This strategy is effective when you want to stop the dialogue and get compliance. However, in the case of RTI, dialogue is critical for building staff buy-in. Because the goal is for the procedures and practices of RTI to become a sustained new paradigm, you'll need deep buy-in for implementation.

Despite the strong links between special education laws and RTI, the premise for implementing RTI has to be built on a much broader and more proactive foundation. Build your base of support around RTI as the right thing to do, not the required thing to do. If you tell your staff that the reason the school is implementing RTI is to comply with special education requirements, then it becomes a special education initiative. Principals who have been extremely successful in implementing RTI have walked a very careful tightrope, right from the start, in positioning this initiative as a joint effort of general education, special education, Title I, and English-language learner (ELL) staff.

> Despite the strong links between special education laws and RTI, the premise for implementing this initiative has to be built on a much broader and more proactive foundation. Build your base of support around RTI as the right thing to do, not the required thing to do.

HISTORY OF RTI

The term *Response to Intervention* is not new; however, it has taken on a new meaning over the past few years. Although the term was previously used in other educational areas including behavior management, in the past 5 years it has been associated most often with early reading. When RTI was associated with behavior modification the term described a process whereby a team of teachers attended a meeting to discuss a problem and select an approach to deal with a student's serious behavior problems. The problem-solving approach is transferable to early reading, where teachers meet to analyze data from curriculum-based measures (CBMs) of early reading skills and decide on an instructional plan to address skill deficits.

Before RTI, few schools conducted data meetings using a problem-solving approach because there were no general education services to offer a struggling reader. The only services generally available for reading help were through special education. Often teachers and parents felt that spending time and energy to qualify a student for special education services was a worthy investment. Yet this system has had many problems. The process of qualifying a student for services is lengthy and often occurs in third grade or later. In order to receive special education services, a family has to go through a long and elaborate qualification process that is procedural in focus and mired in legal hurdles and definitions.

> Before RTI, few schools conducted data meetings using a problem-solving approach because there were no general education services to offer a struggling reader.

But beyond the problem of excessive time for the qualification process, an even more critical problem is that the process occurs too late in a student's school career. In general, students have to wait to fail at reading before they can receive help. Although the signs of difficulty in reading are almost always evident in kindergarten and first grade, until recently the assessments used at these grade levels didn't bring them to light. The largest number of referrals to special education currently occurs in third and fourth grade.

Many educators hail RTI as a mechanism to solve a whole host of problems in how schools deal with reading difficulties. Some of these systemic problems include the following:

- Identification of reading difficulties too late
- Less effective intervention because it was provided too late
- Disproportionate representation of minority students in special education
- Inadequate first teaching for children referred for testing
- Too many unnecessary referrals of students who didn't meet the special education qualification requirements
- Too many students receiving special education services
- Poor communication between general education and special education teachers serving the same student
- Focus on procedures and paperwork rather than prevention and early identification

FORCES DRIVING RTI

Although pressure for a new approach to special education qualification procedures was a significant factor driving RTI, it is not the only factor. Two other forces converged in the same decade and propelled it forward. The low reading scores in schools, along with the controversy over the implementation of the whole language approach, fueled an unparalleled amount of research about early reading. This research was of a different sort than in the past because the National Institutes of Health (NIH) led a push for higher-quality experimental studies that are scientifically based. As the converging findings from this research were released, one important message to educators was that early intervention can prevent reading problems for many students. Another major force was the widespread availability of a new breed of assessments that make early literacy screening and periodic progress monitoring possible. All these initiatives converged in the same decade, and they are influencing each other and RTI.

Special Education Reform Movement

Consider for a moment whether RTI would have engendered the same wide base of support if special education qualification procedures had been structured differently long ago. If schools used federal and state-designated procedures that led to qualifying students earlier for reading services, there would not have been the call for special education reform that drove the widespread support of a better alternative.

In schools, special education qualification practices have been based on what is known as the discrepancy model, an approach to determine whether a student's achievement is different from what would be expected for his or her ability level. Many schools use IQ tests to define the student's ability, and they use scores from achievement assessments to determine how well he or she is reading. Students are qualified to receive special education if their reading achievement is different from their ability level.

Brief History of Special Education Regulations

The legislative guidelines affecting special education were recently overhauled with the revision of the Individuals with Disability Education Act (IDEA) of 1997 to the more recently approved IDEA 2004. This federal act guides states in how to implement special education services, including regulations governing qualification procedures and student rights. With the recently reauthorized IDEA 2004, one of the most widely discussed provisions is the federal government's allowance of RTI. Because RTI is legitimized in this federal law, states and districts now face the challenge of figuring out how to implement it.

IDEA 2004 is the third in a series of major acts in the last 30 years. In the mid-1970s, the first major special education act was released, called the Education for All Handicapped Children Act of 1975. This act granted students with disabilities rights to receive a free and appropriate public education. Although the 1975 act granted education entitlements to children with physical handicaps and a multitude of disabilities that had formerly kept them out of public schools, it ended up serving children with learning disabilities as well.

One ramification of the 1975 act was a huge surge in the number of students qualified with disabilities. Because the act said that all children are entitled to a free and appropriate public education, there was an all-out effort by schools to find students with disabilities so they could be provided a free and appropriate public education. In the decade leading up to 1998, the number of students age 6 to 21 identified for special education increased 38%. Today 12%–14% of students in U.S. schools receive special education services. Recently the increase has been in students who are slightly older.

The increase in 12- to 17-year-olds was 44% (Lyon et al., 2001). Because of the desire to reduce the number of students receiving special education services and the fact that so many are identified late for services, schools are highly motivated to look at RTI as a way to solve both of these problems.

Reauthorization of IDEA 2004

The reauthorization of IDEA affects RTI in a couple of major ways. IDEA 2004 states that use of the discrepancy formula is not required (and is also not abolished). The regulation also permits RTI for qualification. Some educators are pleased with IDEA 2004. However, many claim that it didn't go far enough by deciding not to follow the recommendation of researchers to prohibit the discrepancy formula. Although there is widespread agreement that the discrepancy formula was problematic, there may not have been adequate common ground for exactly what a replacement should look like. Yet the act did open the door for states to determine whether to use the discrepancy formula at all.

> IDEA 2004 states that use of the discrepancy formula is not required (and is also not abolished). The regulation also permits RTI for qualification.

The two sections of the regulations in IDEA 2004 that relate to this question are as follows:

> Notwithstanding section 607 (b), when determining whether a child has a specific learning disability as defined in section 602, a local educational agency shall not be required to take into consideration whether a child has a severe discrepancy between achievement and intellectual ability. (20 U.S.C. 1414(b)(6)(A))

> In determining whether a child has a specific learning disability, a local educational agency may use a process that determines if the child responds to a scientific, research-based intervention as part of the evaluation procedures. (20 U.S.C. 1414(b)(6)(B))

A major impact is that state education agencies cannot force local education agencies to use a discrepancy formula, and in effect RTI can be used as a model of choice. At least two states (West Virginia and Colorado) announced early on that, as of a specific date, they would stop using the discrepancy model. In most states it will not be an either–or approach of using only the discrepancy formula or RTI. Many states advocate multiple sources of data including RTI data, along with selected psychometric diagnostic data, for the qualification process. Some states will still require components of a comprehensive evaluation, but many in the field believe that some of the psychometric testing that traditionally has been done will be scaled back.

Why the Intense Focus on the Discrepancy Formula?

The discrepancy formula was established because a procedure was needed to determine which children qualify for services. Learning disabilities are difficult to diagnose because there is no physical evidence, and the major symptom is unexpected underachievement. The premise is that students who have the capability to do well as measured by IQ yet are not doing well as measured by achievement assessments must have a learning disability that is prohibiting them from acquiring skills from the general education curriculum. It's the discrepancy between IQ and achievement that establishes the disability.

Experts criticize the discrepancy formula for a number of reasons. Is IQ testing accurate? Is it culturally biased? Part of the problem is that an IQ test is measured at a point in time, typically on one day. Even the most highly reliable tests can produce unreliable results when administered only once, which increases the chance of measurement errors. If alternative forms were available, retesting a student's IQ multiple times over a short period of time would increase the likelihood that the test is reliably measuring the student's level of intelligence.

The other criticism is that measuring cognitive processing does not connect to diagnosing the problem or designing an intervention plan. Many experts believe that intelligence is not a predictor of ability to learn to decode. Intelligence may be related to vocabulary and comprehension strategies but not decoding. Many teachers believe that the battery of tests given in schools to evaluate a student for a learning disability is meaningful only to psychologists, not to the teachers who will be working with the student. Too often the test results sit in the child's file and don't inform his or her instructional plan.

The most troubling criticism is that when the discrepancy formula is used, students with difficulties are identified too late. In order to have a gap that meets the state-designated number of standard deviations between IQ and achievement in reading (2.0 in many states), a student has to be old enough to be reading. Because most schools don't expect students to read until the middle to end of first grade, it's extremely difficult to obtain the designated number of standard deviations of discrepancy until they reach second or third grade. Many view the use of the discrepancy model as a basis for special education qualification as a "wait-to-fail" model. According to Dr. Jack Fletcher (2006), a clinical neuropsychologist at the University of Houston, "We have been working with regulations

> The most troubling criticism is that when the discrepancy formula is used, students with difficulties are identified too late.

and procedures that handcuff us and don't enable us to intervene early enough."

As summarized in the NASDSE 2006 publication regarding the work of the National Institute of Child Health & Human Development (NICHD), "One of the most significant implications from this group's work was the nearly irrefutable conclusion that the practice supported by IDEA of using IQ achievement discrepancies to identify SLD (Specific Learning Disability) delays treatment of students beyond the time when interventions are most effective" (NASDSE, 2006, p. 10).

IDEA 2004 Allows Special Education Funds for Prevention

Although the qualification procedure has been the focus of discussion about IDEA 2004, four major changes have resulted from its passage:

- States may not require districts to use IQ tests to identify students as learning disabled.
- States are encouraged to implement RTI as a component of learning disability identification.
- Students cannot be identified for special education without documentation that low achievement is not caused by lack of appropriate instruction.
- Disability categorization must be prevented whenever possible with the use of up to 15% of Part B funds for prevention.

The last one, the allocation of up to 15% of funds for prevention, permits districts to spend money received for special education services to deliver early intervention instruction for students not identified on an Individualized Education Plan (IEP). This includes materials and personnel expenditures.

Before qualification for special education services, the school must provide documentation that the student's low achievement is not caused by a lack of appropriate instruction. Intervention logs are recommended as documentation of the Tier II and Tier III intervention provided (see the case study and Chapter 3 for more information on Tiers I, II, and III). The progress monitoring data provide evidence that the student's skills didn't improve in response to the interventions provided.

Support for RTI From Reading Researchers

As Dr. Sharon Vaughn says, "RTI is an opportunity, not a federal mandate" (Vaughn Gross Center for Reading and Language Arts,

2005, p. 12). It is not required by law, yet it is encouraged and recommended. Consider the broad base of support for this initiative, as evidenced by the number of major policy reports that support it. Over the past 15 years there has been a great deal of research about early reading. It has focused on identifying the skills good readers possess, the skills poor readers lack, and the components of instructional practices that are effective in early reading instruction. The timing of RTI is not a coincidence. It comes on the heels of more than 15 years of reading research, and many of the research findings laid the groundwork.

> *The timing of RTI is not a coincidence. It comes on the heels of more than 15 years of reading research, and many of the research findings laid the groundwork.*

Four important policy reports reference findings that support RTI:

1. *NICHD.* This branch of the NIH provides direction and funding for research studies to discover the skills good readers possess and to uncover the skill deficits of students who do not learn to read well. Although the researchers who direct the programs are affiliated with universities throughout the country, the substantial funding provided by NICHD has positively affected the field of reading education. Two of the relevant major research findings are as follows:

- Reading trajectories are established early and are remarkably stable; students who leave first grade behind in reading nearly always stay behind.
- It takes four times as long to intervene in fourth grade as in late kindergarten to improve a student's skills by the same amount (Lyon, 1997, p. 7).

2. *The National Reading Panel (NRP).* A group of 17 experts was convened for nearly 2 years to distill findings about the most effective practices to teach reading. In 2000 the NRP published a report titled *Report of the National Reading Panel (NRP): Teaching Children to Read.* In September 2001 another publication was released, written in teacher-friendly language to summarize the full report, and it is titled *Put Reading First: The Research Building Blocks for Teaching Children to Read.* The second publication has been distributed in schools throughout the country.

The process the NRP used to study the research is one of the landmark contributions of their work. When the NRP convened, one of their first tasks was to establish criteria about good research, and they decided to include only studies that matched those criteria. The NRP reviewed more than 100,000 studies, using a carefully developed screening procedure, and included in their meta-analysis only the studies that used experimental or quasiexperimental designs and met requirements including minimal sample sizes. Meta-analysis is a technique to quantitatively calculate an overall effect size for a pool of studies. The term "scientifically based reading research" came from the NRP.

Another major contribution of the NRP was to articulate that effective reading instruction should be comprehensive and include instruction in five essential component areas: phonemic awareness, phonics, fluency, vocabulary, and comprehension. The significance of the NRP's work for RTI is that it establishes a gold standard of good curriculum and instruction.

3. *President's Commission on Excellence in Special Education.* President George W. Bush established a committee to recommend improvements to IDEA. In July 2001 this commission published a report titled *A New Era: Revitalizing Special Education for Children and Their Families.* Three major recommendations of the commission are as follows:

- Focus on results, not on process.
- Embrace a model of prevention instead of a model of failure.
- Consider that students with disabilities are involved in general education first and that they also receive extra services.

4. *Fordham Foundation and Progressive Policy Institute: Rethinking Special Education for a New Century.* The Fordham Foundation published a report in 2001 that was positioned as a "state of the union" on special education. The Fordham Foundation's publication was a compilation of articles, the most significant of which claims that many of the difficulties in classifying and defining learning disabilities result from inaccurate assumptions about the causes and characteristics of the disorders. The papers in this publication represent a call to rethink special education. The researchers advocate that sound prevention programs can reduce the number of children needing intensive special education programs and that they should be implemented immediately. In one article, Reid Lyon, Jack Fletcher, et al. (2001) suggest that through early identification and intervention for reading difficulties, the number of children in special education can be reduced by 70%.

These four policy reports are all available online at the Web sites listed in Table 1.2.

Table 1.2 Web Sites for Major Policy Reports

Policy Report	Web Site
National Institutes of Child Health and Human Development, branch of the National Institutes of Health	http://www.nichd.nih.gov/publications/pubs/upload/reading_centers.pdf
Put Reading First: The Research Building Blocks for Teaching Children to Read and the National Reading Panel's publications	http://www.nifl.gov/partnershipforreading/publications/reading_first1.html http://www.nationalreadingpanel.org/Publications/ researchread.htm
President's Commission on Excellence in Special Education	http://www.ed.gov/inits/commissions boards/whspecialeducation/
Fordham Foundation and Progressive Policy Institute: *Rethinking Special Education for a New Century*	http://www.edexcellence.net

Increased Availability of Assessments

Another factor that has contributed to the RTI movement is the release and widespread availability of research-based CBMs. This is important in RTI because in order to evaluate the effectiveness of intervention instruction, one needs periodic progress monitoring assessments. In addition to helping identify who needs intervention, CBM data also help determine the student's rate of progress. CBMs are useful as progress monitoring tools because they are sensitive to growth and can be measured frequently. Progress monitoring data inform decisions about when to adjust instruction, when to stay the course, and when to exit a student from intervention.

> *Progress monitoring data inform decisions about when to adjust instruction, when to stay the course, and when to exit a student from intervention.*

Until 2002, when Reading First was implemented, the use of these measures was more limited than today. Now they are widely available free on the Internet or at a very low cost. CBM passages provide a more research-based approach than local passages to indicate to teachers whether a student can read at grade level. CBMs provide a benchmark that can be used to make decisions about whether a student is reading at grade level based on a score that was derived from large pools of students nationwide.

RELATIONSHIP OF RTI TO OTHER READING SERVICES

How Is RTI Related to Reading First?

Reading First and RTI are completely compatible initiatives. Reading First regulations embody the same principles as RTI, including screening, assessment, and tiers of instruction. Schools that received Reading First grants were told that they were expected to provide small-group instruction for students who are below benchmark.

Although the requirements of Reading First are compatible with RTI, implementation of intervention groups has been slow in Reading First schools. Many schools dedicated their attention in the first couple of years to implementing their new core reading programs, thereby delaying the initiation of Tiers II and III. Because teachers in these schools lacked the foundational knowledge about the acquisition of reading skills, getting to a point of good teaching using the new curriculum took longer than expected.

Guidelines from the U.S. Department of Education's Reading First staff included the message that the core programs must be implemented "with fidelity." Regulations state that funded schools can't layer new programs on top of old practices. The newly purchased core programs are comprehensive, cohesive, and well designed to integrate the five essential components of reading instruction, as framed in the NRP report.

The focus in 2007 has shifted to jump-starting the Tier II and Tier III layers. Teachers are encouraged to analyze the student data and not just plug all students into one intervention program for Tier II and Tier III. Too many schools have purchased intervention programs and are trying to place all below-benchmark students in one of those programs. Confusion reigns. The concepts of differentiation in intervention instruction and fidelity to the core program seem conflicting to teachers. Although the messages are not conflicting, demonstrating why they aren't is complex.

> The concepts of differentiation in intervention instruction and fidelity to the core program seem conflicting to teachers. Although the messages are not conflicting, demonstrating why they aren't is complex.

To make good decisions for differentiated Tier II and Tier III instruction, teachers need to know a great deal about reading instruction. For these students, the instruction in the core program didn't enable them to master the skills. One size doesn't fit all students in reading curricula. Teachers have to use the data to discover which skills the student is lacking. After understanding the core deficits for a student, teachers are prepared to select the best materials available for reteaching the missing skills. To provide effective intervention instruction, teachers must pay more attention to giving the student correction, feedback, and a chance to master the skill in a small group setting.

Confusion About Layering Programs and Materials

In the Reading First Academies, where the U.S. Department of Education trained state leadership teams in the grant request requirements, the topic of prohibiting layering of programs was discussed. The intention was to prohibit use of funds to buy strands of programs and cobble together a core program. For example, they didn't want grant recipients to simply purchase a phonics program and use it in conjunction with some other materials and consider this equivalent to investing in a comprehensive core program designed to carefully integrate instruction in the five essential components. This restriction recognized that the best programs integrate all the components in a well-designed and seamless way, even when the strands are explicitly identified in the teacher's guide. For example, when the teacher's primary purpose is to teach a comprehension strategy during a read-aloud, there may also be a brief vocabulary discussion integrated into a discussion about the story.

The problem now is that many administrators, reading coaches, and teachers in schools that received a Reading First grant are having trouble understanding that they can use intervention programs for Tier II and Tier III that may not cover all five essential components of instruction.

Confusions About the Term Supplemental

The term *supplemental* is used in two ways in Reading First schools. One way refers to using a program to supplement an area of the core that is insufficient for your student population. For example, if your school serves a high ELL population, it may be especially important to use a vocabulary program for 30 minutes a day for all students. In the second sense, some publications call Tier II instruction "supplemental" and Tier III "intervention."

In this book the term "intervention groups" is used for both Tier II and Tier III to avoid confusion and because the focus is on the student's needs, not the programs. Within Tier II groups teachers may gradually try instructional strategies and techniques that are typically associated with Tier III.

How Is RTI Related to Special Education?

Recent criticisms of special education extend well beyond the procedures used to determine eligibility for services. Critics question the effectiveness of the instruction students receive from their special education services. The NASDSE (2006, p. 9) writes, "The benefits of children participating in special education programs compared to their staying in general education programs have been difficult to document unequivocally."

Are the Students on an IEP Included in Three-Tier Intervention?

I recommend providing students who are on an IEP with RTI intervention group instruction in addition to the services for reading they receive in special education. In some schools, the reading intervention students receive in the three-tier model may be more intensive and focused than the instruction they receive in the special education resource room.

It is unrealistic to ask special education teachers to take 10–16 students who are 2–3 years behind their peers and catch them up. These are the students other teachers have been unsuccessful in teaching, and some of these students may have behavior problems as well. Furthermore, schools often ask special education teachers to work with all of these students in one room. That model makes success difficult to achieve. In addition to these difficulties, some special education teachers haven't had as much training in how to teach reading as their general education colleagues.

If RTI is implemented well, then the number of students referred to special education should decrease. This would help because there are too many children in special education to be served with the resources allocated to it. Lyon et al. (2001) suggest that because 80%–90% of students identified as learning disabled were qualified primarily because of difficulties in reading, reducing the number of struggling readers should decrease referrals for special education services.

> Reducing the number of students with reading problems is critical to success, especially in serving middle school students with reading difficulties.

Reducing the number of students with reading problems is critical to success, especially in serving middle school students with reading difficulties. As advocated by a team of reading researchers including Reid Lyon, former director of reading research for the NICHD, and Jack Fletcher, NICHD National Advisory Council,

The goal of remedial reading instruction should be to improve reading skills as quickly as possible so the student can "read to learn" in critical content areas. To accomplish this, students, particularly at older age ranges, require highly intensive and systematic instruction provided in settings characterized by low teacher–student ratios. This can only be done when the potential number of children with reading difficulties has been reduced to manageable levels through early intervention. (Lyon et al., 2001, p. 278)

Although practices that are effective for younger struggling readers are well understood, there are still many questions about effective interventions for middle school students. Studies conducted by Joseph Torgesen and others have shown that intensive interventions can help older children improve their reading accuracy and comprehension, although fluency often remains low. Dr. Torgesen also theorizes that the lack of improvement in fluency may be related to the fact that the struggling older reader has read only a fraction of the cumulative number of words from first grade onward compared with his or her grade-level peers (Lyon, 2001).

If students on an IEP are included in Tier II or Tier III intervention groups, then collaboration between special education and general educators may be encouraged. Currently general education is responsible for the student until there are major problems; then they pass the student to special education. What is needed instead is a system of shared responsibility. When special education and general education work together to implement RTI, the blame, excuses, and finger pointing will disappear.

RTI must be a general education initiative that includes special education as an equal partner. Special education can develop an interest in RTI and bring information to the school. However, special education can't lead the initiative alone. If this initiative resides in special education alone, it will fail. It has to involve general education teachers in the screening, identification, and service delivery systems.

Once RTI is in place, the processes and procedures will serve as a mechanism for qualification of struggling readers into special education. After a student has received repeated rounds of increasingly more intense intervention instruction and his or her skills have failed to improve sufficiently, then the staff can begin to build a case for special education testing. Sometimes these students are called "nonresponders" or "treatment resisters." These terms are misleading because there is nearly always some response to well-taught small-group intervention instruction. "Treatment resister" implies that the student is resisting the treatment rather than that his or her skills are not responding to the instruction provided. I prefer the term "insufficient response." It's a question of degree of response, and I prefer to focus attention on the concept of "insufficient" or "inadequate" response rather than the idea of a nonresponse.

Consider whether the response is what would be expected or sufficient in comparison to the goal. To measure what is expected, compare a student with other students in the same group. If the student in question stands out with a much lower rate of progress than the other students who are receiving the same instruction, this is an insufficient rate of progress. Another consideration is whether the student's rate of progress is sufficient for him or her to reach the benchmark goal; several progress monitoring points falling below the aimline warrants exploring how to intensify instruction.

Grimes and Tilly (2003) suggest that under RTI there are three conditions for eligibility for special education:

- *Insufficient progress:* Previous interventions have not sufficiently improved a student's rate of learning. The criteria of insufficient progress can be met only after several rounds of intervention instruction are provided. After the first round of Tier II is delivered, it is followed by an even more intensive intervention taught well for a reasonable period of time. If the student's scores do not show adequate gains, often in comparison to others who received the same intervention, then the student can be deemed to have made an insufficient level of progress.
- *Level of performance:* The student's performance remains significantly below that of peers or identified grade-level standards. To be considered for special education services, a student would need to be reading well below benchmark or unable to demonstrate mastery of the prereading skills of his peers.
- *Instructional needs:* Additional resources are needed to enhance the student's learning that are beyond what can be provided in general education. Another possible reason to refer a student is if teachers determine that the interventions needed are too demanding to be implemented without access to special education funding and resources.

It is critical that special education and general education become a more seamless series of services available to students. Some schools view special education as Tier IV after a student's skills do not improve adequately in Tiers II and III.

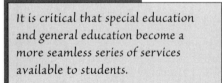

It is critical that special education and general education become a more seamless series of services available to students.

When IDEA 2004 allowed RTI as a qualification procedure for special education, the door was opened for this initiative to reform special education. Additionally, by dedicating up to 15% of special education funding to providing instruction that prevents referrals for IEPs, the federal government has enabled states to outline procedures that are significantly different from those required in the past. This change in the federal provision is an opportunity to integrate the service delivery model in schools so that Tiers II and III are aligned to provide help immediately and monitor a student's progress. These changes should also create a streamlined and much more effective type of instruction that is truly "special" education for students whose skills don't improve sufficiently in the tiers of services available in general education.

Setting the Stage for RTI

Children are working at levels in which they can be successful. It is great for their self-confidence. They have a positive attitude about reading.

—Kindergarten teacher

Leading an RTI initiative is no small undertaking. The magnitude of the implementation effort lies not only in the quantity of work but also in the significant leadership and strategic planning skills needed. At a meeting of a planning committee of the West Virginia RTI Project, one of the regional representatives described the complex leadership requirements. He said that the best implementations he has observed were facilitated by leaders who are as savvy as the most astute politicians. Good RTI leaders know how to

- Assemble a good team.
- Make wise decisions about how to proceed.
- Know when to publicize and when to be quiet.
- Create unity so that all the pieces fit together.
- Run interference when key players begin to resist the initiative.
- Make decisions in a very deliberate manner.
- Facilitate consensus that this initiative is good for students.

This regional representative continued with a clear description of one school he serves. He said that a special education director at the district office took a limited pool of funds, cherry-picked a strong principal, and had a successful pilot site in place before anyone knew what was happening. When the district Title I director resisted the initiative, this leader was in a better position to run interference to protect his plans because success had already been demonstrated in his pilot site.

MOTIVATING CHANGE

Implementing any major change in a school is difficult. It is wise to anticipate that there will be reluctant or resistant teachers. Some teachers insist that their students are reading very well, and other teachers don't want to implement the three-tier framework because they don't want to vary their own approach to teaching reading. Occasionally a reluctant teacher simply doesn't want to work harder to analyze data and collaborate more with colleagues. Because of the difficulty of implementing RTI, a principal needs to determine his or her capacity to lead change amid resistance or reluctance.

Because of the level of work and change needed to implement RTI, a district should not launch an RTI initiative without a great deal of consideration. Therefore, it is important to think in advance about why the school or district should take on this process. To make RTI work, the staff must be committed to the idea, and that commitment comes more easily when teachers believe that students aren't learning to read as well as they could be. Teachers want their students to do well, so the more clearly you can demonstrate how RTI will help their students, the more buy-in there will be among the staff. The implementation will be smoother if the staff believes that the current level of performance is too low and that therefore something must change.

Highlighting Unacceptable Student Scores

One way to demonstrate that the current student reading level is unacceptably low is to compare your school's scores with those of a comparison group. The comparison scores can be an average for your district or taken from selected schools in your district or a school with a similar student population. The unacceptable level of performance can be the school's overall reading level, or it may be only one particular grade level or a specific subpopulation of students in the school. For example, your data analysis may show that the number of students receiving special education services for reading is extraordinarily high compared with the national, state, or district average. On the other hand, your data may show that the number of minority students with low reading scores is disproportionate and unacceptable. Consider which comparison will motivate your teachers to act. One principal reported that his teachers didn't want their school to be one of the bottom schools in the district ranking by student reading scores, so that's the comparison group he chose to highlight.

Compliance With a Grant Requirement

When a school has accepted a grant with nonnegotiable requirements, the debate about implementation is narrowed to how to implement rather than whether to do so. In Reading First schools, at times it has been helpful for principals to state that certain procedures are required by the grant; for example, Reading First schools are required to administer an early literacy screening instrument, identify students who need intervention, and provide small-group intervention instruction in addition to the core reading instruction. Even if the staff is not pleased with some of the requirements, the advantages can make them worthwhile. Reading First schools are able to fund the position of a reading coach and buy new materials that they otherwise would not have been able to afford. In my experience most teachers in Reading First schools appreciate the professional development, help from the reading coach, funding for substitutes for increased collaboration time, and the abundance of new materials. When a teacher complains about the extra work or how difficult these new practices are, it's easy for a principal to point out all these benefits.

A Leader's Passion

Other than compliance with grant requirements, a common impetus for implementing RTI is when a principal or superintendent launches this initiative as a way to improve reading scores. The superintendent's support is helpful; the principal's commitment is essential. The superintendent can start the initiative, but one way or another, the principals must be brought on board. Principals, not the superintendent, are in the position to ensure that the teachers are looking at the data and teaching intervention groups daily. It is not uncommon for one principal in the district to be the initial leader who

> The superintendent's support is helpful; the principal's commitment is essential.

carries the idea up to the superintendent. In that case, gaining the superintendent's support is critical to spread the practice to the other schools in the district.

Some schools have highlighted the excessive number of students in special education as a motivation for implementing RTI. At one school in West Virginia, the principal is the motivational leader behind the implementation of RTI, and one of his stated goals is to reduce the number of students on an Individualized Education Plan. This principal learned about RTI and got his superintendent's backing. Shortly thereafter the superintendent resigned, and it took the principal nearly a year to sell the idea to the new superintendent. Fortunately, there was a special education teacher on the board who helped convince the new superintendent. This principal's passion for RTI was infectious and set the stage for his staff to agree that the special education population is too high and has to be reduced. During a conversation he said, "I know that we live in a rural area where kids come in with very little literacy preparation. Yet there is just no way that 29% of our population needs special education."

GETTING READY TO LAUNCH RTI

Collecting Baseline Data

Although it is possible to initially highlight the need for RTI with state assessment data for reading at third grade, eventually baseline data for each grade level will be needed. These data will serve as a measure of the starting point before RTI is implemented, so it is better to collect a baseline using the same assessment instrument that will be used later. Many schools collect data in May, at the end of the school year, before launching RTI in the fall.

Grounding the Initiative in Research

> When it comes to deciding how to teach reading, decisions cannot be based on personal opinions about best teaching practices.

Over the last few decades, there have been way too many ill-fated initiatives in early reading instruction, causing wide pendulum swings in practice. During the initial RTI implementation is a good time to align instruction with scientifically based reading research. When it comes to deciding how to teach reading, decisions cannot be based on personal opinions about best teaching practices. Aligning with the research means making a commitment to follow recommendations from eminent research reviews such as the National Reading Panel report.

It is important to guide the staff's commitment to do what works rather than what they like. The following example from a school in Kansas, where RTI has been implemented for a couple of years, demonstrates the significance of teachers committing to teach what works. The principal uses a goal-setting process with his staff called SMART, developed by Conzemius and O'Neill (2001). SMART is an acronym that describes five characteristics of goal setting:

S = Strategic and specific

M = Measurable

A = Attainable

R = Result oriented

T = Time bound

This principal asks teachers to establish SMART goals and to track progress toward goals through weekly e-mails to him. One of his second-grade teachers named Stefanie established a goal to reduce the number of students reading below benchmark from 70% at the beginning of the year to less than 20%, as measured by a curriculum-based measure (CBM). One of Stefanie's weekly journal entries shows her reflections:

> At the beginning of this process, the question I wanted to answer was this: How do we best address the lack of Oral Reading Fluency gain from the first DIBELS [Dynamic Indicators of Basic Early Literacy Skills] testing window to the middle testing window? Since my horrible realization that teaching the way I have always taught would no longer work, I have been forced to take a deeper look at my students and their data. . . . I have taken on the challenging task of teaching a new reading program that is researched based, but by no means "fun." With that said, I feel that the progress is slow but sure.

This teacher is using the data to select the curriculum her students need.

At a district in New York that implemented RTI in all of its elementary schools in the first 2 years and moved to include middle schools in the third year, the K–12 English language arts and reading coordinator reflects on the use of CBMs and diagnostic screeners. She says, "The result of having a more diagnostic assessment has meant that the students' needs are controlling the curriculum, not the teacher's favorite activities."

Knowing the research helps in more ways than guiding best instructional practices. It also helps establish a goal for the school's expected success. As reported in an article in *American Educator* (Torgesen, 2004), early intervention studies show that 95% or more of students can read successfully with strong early identification and intervention. Torgesen reports that all but 1%–4% of students can reach benchmark with early intervention in place. These findings are useful for principals reminding their staff to set high expectations for the success of *all* students in reading.

Principal's Role

What does it mean to be an instructional leader of RTI implementation in a school? Leading RTI is too important to delegate to an assistant principal or reading coach. The minute a principal designates an assistant to be the leader and spokesperson for an initiative, the message sent to staff is that the process is a low priority. It is critical for the principal to keep talking about RTI in staff and grade-level meetings.

The principal must lead a variety of tasks:

- Selecting the right staff to be involved in the process
- Motivating the staff by demonstrating how this initiative is good for students
- Managing teachers who resist RTI
- Establishing a set of processes and procedures to make decisions about students based on the data
- Planning and attending professional development activities
- Participating actively in data analysis meetings
- Evaluating the effectiveness of the tiers of instruction

The staff will take more interest if it is clear that this initiative is the top priority for the school. Often principals launch so many initiatives that the staff feels their time and attention are pulled in too many directions.

COMMUNICATION PLAN

One way in which a principal can demonstrate commitment to RTI is to keep talking about it. Until there is staff buy-in, align talking points closely with core beliefs of RTI. Promote the idea that prevention is better for students than remediation. Remind teachers that the early literacy screener is needed to identify which students need intervention. After there is buy-in, the principal's communication can change from promoting the belief in RTI to asking questions about the processes teachers are expected to use. How are data used to inform instructional decisions? What percentage of students are currently at benchmark? How many students have moved from below benchmark into the benchmark range since the beginning of the year? How many students are receiving intervention instruction at this time? Ask questions to indicate what you expect them to be doing.

At the initiation of RTI, the principal is the main spokesperson to articulate the purpose of this initiative. Some communication points to consider at the outset are listed here:

- *This is a joint initiative of all who serve struggling readers, including general education and special education teachers.* RTI is a golden opportunity for a principal to align the often compartmentalized ways in which struggling readers have been served in schools for too long. This initiative can be used as a way to coordinate general educators, special educators, Title I teachers, and English as a second language (ESL) staff under one umbrella. It's possible to align everyone by using the same early literacy screening data, discussing student progress as a team, and making decisions about students with a view toward coordinated service delivery, rather than disjointed interventions from teachers who rarely communicate or collaborate.
- *There will be universal screening of all K–3 students three times a year.* Screening is a critical part of an RTI model, and it is good for all students. Not only does it provide the data to identify which students need extra instruction, it also enables teachers to confirm that the benchmark students remain above benchmark and don't lose ground over the year.
- *All below-benchmark students are entitled to small-group intervention instruction.* Because of tight resources, some schools decide to provide intervention only to the students identified with the instructional recommendation of "intensive." It is important not to leave out the "strategic" students because failure to serve them now may mean that they will need more intensive intervention later, after losing critical time at the early point when intervention is most effective and efficient.
- *Intervention groups are skill groups, and their instruction is focused.* These intervention groups must be viewed as skill groups, not ability groups. The instruction should be focused on the skills that the group has not mastered and will not necessarily cover all the components of reading taught during the core instruction time (known as the five essential components of reading instruction).

- *Decisions about membership in flexible groups will be based on the benchmark and progress monitoring data.* Students will enter groups when their scores indicate they are at risk and will remain in these groups only as long as needed to raise their skills to benchmark levels. Students exit intervention groups after multiple consecutive scores at or above benchmark. Therefore, the membership of the groups is flexible, based on progress monitoring data.
- *Groups will be small enough for instruction to be effective.* Intervention instruction ideally is taught in groups with no more than five students, and preferably only three. Commit to serve students in groups that are small enough for the teacher to give corrective feedback to all the students for each error they make.
- *A student's background will be considered in determining how to help, never as an excuse for low reading ability.* Adopt a culture of no excuses. It's helpful to know that a student hears very little sophisticated oral language at home, or his or her family speaks a language other than English. Accept that many things that affect a student's readiness to read aren't controlled by the school. Acknowledging that factors affect the school's task of teaching reading is fine, yet the school's culture prohibits viewing these considerations as a justification for why a student can't read.

> Your staff needs to believe that RTI is here to stay and is not the "idea du jour."

- *Implementing RTI is a 3- to 5-year effort.* Your staff needs to believe that RTI is here to stay and is not the "idea du jour." Too often in the past teachers have been rewarded for waiting as new efforts died out. Minimize the other initiatives that will compete for the teachers' time and attention.

PLANNING AN RTI INITIATIVE

Implementation in Phases

One of the most critical decisions a principal makes is the number of grade levels to implement in the first year. Rolling out RTI to all grade levels to the same degree in the first year is risky. Consider carefully how much the school can handle the first year and think of this as a phase-by-phase implementation. Sometimes schools collect data for all grades in the first year but implement intervention groups only for one or two grade levels that year. Some steps precede others and set the stage for implementation of later steps.

- *Start with universal screening as the first step.* The school will need baseline data for a whole host of reasons, not the least of which is to motivate change.
- *Limit the number of grade levels for the initial year.* It is far better in the first year to focus and get results than to take on too many grade levels and have mixed results. Don't take on kindergarten through fifth grade at an elementary school or sixth through eighth grade at a middle school in the first year. Many times elementary schools launch both kindergarten and first grade the initial year, which usually can be managed well. The problem with taking on too many grade levels is that you risk poor implementation at every grade level. When the results are lukewarm, it's too easy for the naysayers to claim, "We tried this, and it doesn't work." It takes time for teachers to understand what they are doing and to feel competent in using data-driven intervention groups. It's far better to implement a bit more slowly and allow the momentum to build.

> It is far better in the first year to focus and get results than to take on too many grade levels and have mixed results.

- *Start with the lowest grade level and work up in following years.* Occasionally an administrator wants to start with third grade because that's the year of state assessments or fourth grade because it's the elementary school's final chance to catch these students up before they move to the middle school. Although no one wants to ignore the struggling readers at the later grade levels, the school needs to build a firewall to stop the large number of students getting to fourth grade with inadequate reading skills. It is best for a district to start at kindergarten and dedicate available resources to fully implement RTI at kindergarten before moving up the grade levels. Results are evident earlier in kindergarten and first grade because there are fewer deficit skill areas to improve, and the data are more sensitive to change. It's possible to get more than 90% of students in kindergarten and first grade to benchmark in the first year of RTI with aggressive implementation. There's nothing like success to build momentum for later grades, where improvements are not as immediate. The number of hours of instruction needed to remediate a student in fourth grade and beyond is substantial, and results don't show right away. Teachers need to believe that this works, based on success at earlier grade levels.

- *Select a few schools in the district to pilot RTI.* When the initiative is led from the district level, it is best to carefully select a school with a high likelihood of success to serve as a pilot. Choose a school where the principal is an instructional leader and will be a good advocate for RTI among the other principals and where there are plenty of teachers who are willing and able to implement this new approach. Of course, the success will not be as meaningful if the pilot site is a school with a reputation of doing everything well or one whose students are among the highest scoring in the district. It is less effective to select one turnkey teacher at a grade level to attend professional development training with the assumption that he or she can show the other teachers in their building what to do. Training all the teachers in the pilot site buildings is preferable so that they can collaborate from the outset.

- *Reassign staff if needed to have the right resources focused for success.* If the reading coach in your building is serving kindergarten through fifth grade, consider reallocating the coach's time to fewer grade levels. The same is true of intervention teachers or aides. Focus as much staff as possible on the grade level(s) where you are implementing RTI.

- *Decide on goals for year one.* Many schools focus the entire first year on mastering the assessment and data management piece. There are tradeoffs to this approach. Although it makes the second year smoother, the downside is that another entire year has elapsed before data analysis and intervention groups are launched in those grade levels. That's an entire year for teachers to feel annoyed about assessing without doing anything with the data. It may be advisable to use assessment teams to collect baseline data, and then train teachers to assess just before rolling out the three-tier framework at a grade level.

- *Add an intervention block into the master schedule for the focus grade levels.* Anything on the master schedule is considered a priority and is more likely to be done. If intervention time isn't added to the master schedule, the principal is asking teachers to figure out how to fit intervention time into their already crowded schedule. Scheduling an intervention block facilitates monitoring by the principal and reading coach, who can walk down the grade-level hallway and glance in classrooms to see whether students are in small intervention groups. Preparing the master schedule is difficult, often causing more dissension than nearly anything else. Some buildings gather staff in the same room with posterboards and self-stick notes to see how to schedule a 90-minute block for language arts, a 30-minute reading intervention block, a math block, and time for other classes such as physical education and music (see sample master schedule in Table 2.1).

Table 2.1 Sample Master Schedule With Intervention Blocks

95% GROUP INC.

Sample School Master Schedule

Time	Kindergarten	First Grade	Second Grade	Third Grade	Coach
8:00–8:15		Homeroom	Homeroom	Homeroom	Prep
8:15–8:40	Core Reading Block	Core Reading Block	Core Reading Block	**In Class Intervention**	Observe Core Reading Block
8:40–9:15	**In Class Intervention**	Core Reading Block	Core Reading Block	Core Reading Block	Observe Core Reading Block
9:15–9:35	Core Reading Block	Core Reading Block	Core Reading Block	Core Reading Block	Observe Core Reading Block
9:35–9:55	Recess	Spelling	**In Class Intervention**	Recess	Prep
10:00–10:15	Instructional Time	Recess	Recess	Block 1	Prep
10:15–10:55	Instructional Time	**In Class Intervention**	Music, Arts, and Crafts	1 Math | 2 Science & Social Science - Benchmark & Intervention Groups	First Grade Intervention
10:40–11:25	Instructional Time	Math	Planning Time and Specials	(Block 1 continues)	Third Grade and Second Grade Intervention
11:25–11:45	Instructional Time	Music, Arts, and Crafts	Lunch	Lunch / Block 2	Third Grade and Second Grade Intervention
11:50–12:55	Lunch; Instructional Time	Lunch; Planning Time and Specials	Science and Social Science Pull Out Intervention	2 Science & Social Science - Benchmark & Intervention Groups | 2 Math	Third Grade and Second Grade Intervention; Lunch
1:00–1:25	Pull Out Intervention	Language Arts	Language Arts and Spelling	**In Class Intervention**	Kindergarten Intervention
1:30–1:45	Instructional Time	Recess	Recess	Recess	Prep
1:50–2:55	Recess; Instructional Time	Science and Social Science Pull Out Intervention; Language Arts	Math	Planning Time and Specials	First Grade Intervention; Third Grade Intervention

- *Involve the right players from the start.* Form an RTI committee with carefully selected members. Consider which staff needs to be involved and increase ownership and buy-in by engaging them from the beginning. Consider including the special education director, Title I coordinator, and ESL coordinator. Often principals include a representative teacher from each grade level so they can take information back to grade-level meetings, including even the grade levels not yet implementing. Whether the representative is the grade-level team leader depends on whether that person is an early adopter. Select committee members who are enthusiastic about this initiative. It's important to encourage both bottom-up and top-down approaches for RTI.

- *Identify teachers who are early adopters and nurture their work to promote model classrooms and early success stories.* Because one of the easiest ways to convince a reluctant teacher is by sharing improved student data from a peer's classroom, identifying and supporting the early adopters is critical. Even though at first there may not be complete buy-in among all the teachers, go with the early adopters; their success will help bring the others around. The early adopters become your best advocates. Identify at least one teacher per grade level to demonstrate early success and provide a model classroom for others to observe. Consider allowing a reasonable amount of time for reluctant teachers to come around. However, do not allow them to apply negative pressure or stand in the way of the early implementers. For the rare teacher who continues to refuse to implement by the end of the first year, offer them a transfer to another grade level or another school.

> Even though at first there may not be complete buy-in among all the teachers, go with the early adopters; their success will help bring the others around.

- *Identify a reading expert to serve as the RTI coordinator and define that teacher's role carefully.* Find a reading specialist who can serve as your advisor, data coordinator, and peer coach to the teachers. In Reading First schools there is typically a reading coach. In other schools this may be a Title I teacher, reading specialist, or special education teacher. The RTI coordinator must have a strong understanding of reading, collaborate well with teachers, be respected by the teachers, and like working with data. Define the role carefully and make that role clear to all the staff. Some duties include managing the assessment team, managing data, serving as a liaison between grade-level teams and the principal, and coaching and mentoring teachers as they place students in groups and determine instruction. If possible, reduce the coordinator's responsibilities with students so that 25%–50% of her time is available for coordinator duties. It's helpful if the coordinator can attend the grade-level team meetings for the grades that are implementing RTI (see Table 2.2 for a sample of job responsibilities).

Table 2.2   Job Responsibilities of RTI Coach or Coordinator

Important prerequisite skills	• Clearly understands reading development and effective instructional practices to teach reading to struggling readers • Collaborates well with teachers • Enjoys working with data

Responsibilities of RTI coordinator	• Administration of assessments
	  ○ Oversees the assessment calendar
	  ○ Orders assessment materials
	  ○ Organizes storage system for student scoring booklets
	  ○ Manages the assessment team (if there is one)
	  ○ Organizes schedule for rotating substitutes during assessment periods
	  ○ Trains teachers in how to administer assessments
	  ○ Provides review sessions on critical administration rules and procedures before each benchmark period
	• Data collection and reporting
	  ○ Coordinates collection of data from assessment teams and classroom teachers
	  ○ Distributes reports to teachers
	  ○ Coordinates distribution of data to special education, Title I, speech-language pathology, and English as a second language leaders on students they serve
	  ○ Prepares data notebook for principal and updates it frequently
	• Coordination of RTI processes
	  ○ Attends grade-level team meetings to coordinate RTI processes across grade levels
	  ○ Serves as liaison between the principal and teachers on the RTI initiative

Additional responsibilities of RTI coach	• Data analysis
	  ○ Meets with teachers individually or in grade-level teams to help interpret data
	  ○ Instructs teachers in data analysis procedures, including item analysis on student probes for error patterns
	  ○ Helps teachers place students in intervention groups and define focus of instruction for each group
	• Planning intervention instruction for each group
	  ○ Assists teachers in preparing materials and strategies for each group
	• Instructional coach
	  ○ Models effective intervention group instruction for teachers
	  ○ Observes teachers instructing intervention groups and provides feedback and coaching

- *Expect classroom teachers to provide intervention instruction.* Once baseline data are available, estimate the resources needed to serve below-benchmark students. In some schools a cultural shift is needed in order for classroom teachers to view themselves as interventionists. I recommend that even if your school has plenty of reading specialists or instructional aides to teach all the small groups, expect each classroom teacher to teach at least one intervention group. Many times classroom teachers view a student's qualification for special education as an event that shifts responsibility for that student's reading outcome to the special education teacher. Special education is too often viewed as a place students go rather than an instructional process. Avoid repeating this scenario. With RTI, classroom teachers learn to collaborate as members of a team to evaluate each struggling reader and learn to use assessment data to inform instructional decisions. Learning how to deliver differentiated, focused instruction in these small groups provides professional growth that will forever improve the teacher's reading instruction.

Designing an Assessment Plan

Several key decisions must be made in the design of the assessment plan for RTI. These decisions include selecting the assessment instruments, determining whether to make or buy access to data management services, establishing an assessment calendar, and determining whether a limited team or all classroom teachers will administer the screening.

Select an Early Literacy Screening Instrument

One of the most critical decisions a principal or district leader makes is which early literacy screening assessment instrument to use. It's a crucial decision simply because it's disruptive to change assessments midstream. All you need to do is talk with the staff of any Reading First school in Illinois to understand the consequences of a switch. The Illinois State Department of Education decided to use a state-designed early literacy screening tool called Illinois Snapshots of Early Literacy (ISEL) as the screening assessment for Illinois Reading First schools. Hundreds of teachers were trained, and they collected data the first year. After a federal review at the end of the first year, the ISEL was disallowed, and they switched to DIBELS. The disruption created by the switch in assessment instruments set the schools back in their implementation of Reading First.

If a school switches assessment instruments during RTI implementation, some consequences include the following:

- Loss of a comparable set of baseline data used as a starting point before implementation of RTI
- Substantial duplication of time to retrain teachers on a second screening assessment
- Confusion for students in becoming familiar with new testing routines
- Mixed signals to teachers about assessment

Because it's important to select the right assessment tool the first time, it's worth investing time and energy to make this decision wisely. Several helpful resources are as follows:

- Reading First Academy Assessment Committee: http://oregon readingfirst.uoregon.edu/assessment.php
- National Center on Student Progress Monitoring: http://www .studentprogress.org
- Research Institute on Progress Monitoring: http://www.progress monitoring.org

Several important criteria in selecting a good screening assessment include that the assessment is effective and accurate in identifying the right students and that its effectiveness is supported by scientific research. Principals should insist that any screening instrument be backed with an extensive research base demonstrating its validity and reliability. Good screening instruments will not underidentify or overidentify students for assessment. If the screening instrument has benchmarks that are too high, students who need intervention will slip through unnoticed until they fail to read later. If the threshold for identification for help is too low, the intervention delivery system will be overtaxed with students who would have read without this extra help.

Another criterion of a good screening instrument is that it takes little time to assess a student. An efficient screening instrument helps schools dedicate minimum staff time for assessment and maximum time for instruction. The purpose of the screening instrument is to tell you who is behind, in as efficient a manner as possible. However, it doesn't always tell you what to teach. Informal phonological awareness or phonics assessments can help identify a student's specific skill deficits.

The time it takes to administer screening instruments varies a great deal. DIBELS takes 3–8 minutes to assess a student at the benchmark screening. Many other early literacy screening instruments take 20–45 minutes per student, including the Texas Primary Reading Inventory, the ISEL, and Virginia's Phonological Awareness and Literacy Screening.

One of the most important criteria in selecting an assessment screening instrument is that progress monitoring forms are included. The availability of alternative forms enables teachers to repeatedly assess the indicator, after intervention has started, in order to track the effectiveness of instruction. The repeated assessment of a CBM serves a different purpose than other assessments teachers give across the school year. Assessments such as end-of-unit tests or weekly spelling tests assess different skills on each test. This purpose is different from that of repeatedly administering a CBM indicator to measure growth in the same skill, such as words read correctly per minute in comparable passages. The graphing of the progress monitoring data is what makes CBMs powerful. Doug Fuchs, from Vanderbilt University, summarizes the scientific research of the use of CBMs. Fuchs writes that there is evidence of "strong effects on students' reading, spelling, and mathematics achievement" when teachers rely on CBM progress monitoring, especially when they graph those scores, to plan their instruction (Fuchs & Fuchs, 2006, p. 4).

Select a Data Management System

Two options for managing the data are subscribing to a service to collect and report assessment data or creating your own management system. A number of commercially-available data management systems collect and organize student data and provide a set of reports. For example, if your school uses DIBELS, two services are available. The University of Oregon's data management system costs $1 per student per year (at the time of press), or a somewhat higher fee for CBM data in AIMSweb, another system. Schools can also develop their own spreadsheet or data management systems. A subscription to one of these systems is well worth the cost. Allow time to sign up for the subscription and to establish passwords and levels of authority that specify who has access to which data. Plan ahead to get this all set up before assessment begins so that once the benchmark data are collected, they can be input right away.

Although schools can design their own spreadsheets to collect data, format the reports according to their interests, and create special graphs and charts to highlight trends in the student data, doing so may not merit the effort. The information is more meaningful than ever before as the University of Oregon has added more valuable reports to the system that are increasingly difficult to replicate. For example, the Effectiveness of Core Instruction report is used to track the effectiveness of the instructional program. The analysis is calculated by determining how many students moved up a level, stayed the same, or slipped down one instructional recommendation category (e.g., from benchmark to strategic). What makes this report difficult to duplicate is that the effect of mobility is neutralized by the inclusion only of students enrolled at the beginning and end of the period; tracking this effect in a spreadsheet would be difficult.

Establish an Assessment Calendar

It is helpful for all teachers to be on the same cycle for collecting progress monitoring data. One benefit of a common monitoring calendar is that principals know when data will be fresh for grade-level meetings or for planning the timing of outside consultant visits. For example, if progress monitoring occurs every 3 weeks, there will be three data points after 9 weeks of intervention instruction. Three progress monitoring points are helpful for looking closely at the rate of progress to determine whether to intensify a student's instruction. Every 9 weeks is a good time to begin planning meetings to review progress of all students receiving intervention.

Many schools establish an assessment calendar in the spring before the year starts or just before the beginning of the school year. Generally they select a 2-week period in August or September, depending on the start of school, as their fall benchmark assessment window. Although it's important to launch intervention groups as early as possible, it's wise to allow a couple of weeks for students to get back into the routine of school. Most schools have a 2-week window, which allows enough time for teachers to complete screening by assessing a couple of students each day or enough time for a team to spend a couple days per grade level. The winter benchmark window typically begins the second week of January, and the third benchmark can be scheduled in mid- to late May.

The appropriate frequency of progress monitoring depends on several considerations. There is a tradeoff. Frequent progress monitoring provides more data points to increase the reliability of the trend line of progress. Another advantage of more frequent assessment is that it is more likely that fresh data will be available when teams meet to make instructional decisions about a student. However, too frequent progress monitoring takes valuable time away from instruction. In DIBELS there are 20 alternative forms, so weekly progress monitoring will use them up in about half of the school year. One common practice is to assess the lowest-performing students, those identified with an instructional recommendation of "intensive," every 2 weeks and the other students every 3 weeks. Some schools decide to progress monitor monthly in the first year as they learn to use the data and organize the instructional delivery system. Regardless of what's on the calendar, teachers should be encouraged to progress monitor any student more often when there are concerns or when the student's scores are erratic.

When establishing the assessment calendar, pay careful attention to key dates such as state testing week, inservices or holidays, and parent conferences and the number of instructional weeks from one progress monitoring to another. Teachers become more agitated about testing if it occurs when there are conflicting demands on their time. Once you've figured out the calendar, publish it so all teachers can adequately prepare for the weeks to assess. An example of an assessment calendar is provided in Table 2.3.

Table 2.3   Example of an RTI Assessment Calendar

	Benchmark	Progress Monitoring
Fall Benchmark	9/11 to 9/22	
Progress monitoring #1		10/9 to 10/13
Progress monitoring #2		10/30 to 11/3
Progress monitoring #3		11/27 to 12/1
Progress monitoring #4		12/18 to 12/22
Winter Benchmark	1/15 to 1/26	
Progress monitoring #5		2/12 to 2/16
Progress monitoring #6		3/5 to 3/9
Progress monitoring #7		4/2 to 4/6
Progress monitoring #8		4/23 to 4/27
Spring Benchmark	5/14 to 5/25	

Determine Who Administers Assessments

In addition to selecting which screening instrument to adopt, one other strategic decision is whether classroom teachers will assess their own students or an assessment team will do some or all of the testing. This decision is strategic because both approaches have various implications. Many researchers believe that using an assessment team may provide more accurate data because the team is more objective and delivers the assessment more often, which improves consistency and interrater reliability. However, in the team approach teachers are less likely to fully understand and use the data if they don't give the assessment. Early literacy screening data are supposed to be formative data, or data that are used to make decisions throughout the year rather than measure end-of-the-year outcomes.

One concern with teachers assessing their own classrooms is the potential to score their own students higher than an assessment team member would. Although it's understandable that teachers are under pressure to deliver high student scores, it would be unethical for a teacher to intentionally skew her own students' results and thereby deny a student intervention instruction that may be needed.

Many schools combine these approaches as a way to have the best of both worlds. They use an assessment team to collect the baseline data when they first implement RTI. Then they train the teachers over time to administer the assessment screening. Assessment team members often include school psychologists, speech–language pathologists, reading coaches, the assistant principal or director of curriculum, and one teacher from some or all grade levels.

A couple of other approaches achieve the desired balance between the accurate collection of data and the benefits of teacher involvement in assessing their own students. One plan is to have assessment teams administer the three benchmark assessments and classroom teachers deliver the progress monitoring assessments. Another option is for the teachers to do all the testing and an assessment team to retest with a progress monitoring probe approximately 10% of students just after the benchmark testing to confirm that the scores are within a very narrow range of the teacher results. It is preferable to retest from the very beginning so that it doesn't appear to be in response to an issue of overstated scores. Either the random retesting or the team assessment at benchmark times will provide reliability in the data without taking away the benefits gained from teachers assessing their own students.

I recommend that all classroom teachers be trained in administration procedures and administer the assessment before the beginning of the second year. In order to gain full buy-in and complete implementation of data-driven instruction, it is critically important for teachers to administer the screening assessment. Teachers make more perceptive observations about students' strengths and weaknesses while administering the assessments, and they never quite appreciate or accept the data in the same way when provided data rather than administering the assessment themselves. Nothing matches the experience of watching the student make the errors. Teacher observation is especially critical because the purpose of these data is to inform the teacher about student needs. An early literacy assessment screening does not have the same function as high-stakes testing, where the purpose of the data is to report competency levels to such stakeholders as parents and the state department of education. With screening instruments, it's not about reporting the data as much as it is about using the data to inform instruction.

> Teachers make more perceptive observations about students' strengths and weaknesses while administering the assessments, and they never quite appreciate or accept the data in the same way when provided data rather than administering the assessment themselves.

Despite the many benefits of teachers administering the assessment screening, after the first benchmark some teachers will complain that assessment takes a lot of time away from instruction. As part of the teacher training in administering the assessment, include shadow scoring so that two teachers can screen together and compare scores. This not only improves the teacher's confidence but also increases scoring accuracy. Shadow scoring and random retesting help reveal misunderstandings about scoring rules.

Chapter 3 explores how to help teachers organize the instructional delivery system so that once the data are analyzed, students can be placed in intervention groups.

Staff to Assist With RTI

A new job position in the field of early reading is quickly gaining momentum. Many schools have created the position of a reading coach whose job is focused on helping teachers improve their instruction. Many schools that don't have the funding for full-time reading coaches are creating a part-time position of RTI coordinator. The role of each is discussed in this section.

Role of a Reading Coach

In *The Reading Coach: A How-To Manual for Success,* Hasbrouck and Denton (2006, p. 2) offer a definition of coaching as "a cooperative, ideally collaborative relationship, with parties mutually engaged in efforts to provide better services for students." What makes the role of a reading coach challenging is that the coach is a peer trying to help colleagues improve their reading instruction. When the principal doesn't provide clarity about the coach's role, it may be nearly impossible for a coach to be effective.

The role of the reading coach often includes the following responsibilities:

- Observe teachers providing reading lessons and provide feedback
- Model good teaching instruction and lessons
- Provide professional development for teachers, including teaching workshops, facilitating grade-level meetings, and organizing book studies
- Meet one on one to coach teachers
- Help teachers manage assessment data and interpret results
- Show teachers how to organize materials and plan lessons
- Advise the principal in areas related to reading instruction

One of the most important principles about the reading coach's role is that it is not supervisory or evaluative. The coach is there to help and support teachers in providing the most effective reading instruction possible for their students. Coaches have to build trusting relationships with teachers before coaching can occur. When teachers don't understand the role or trust the coach, they may reject his or her suggestions or view the coach as an adversary.

Role of an RTI Coordinator

In schools where there is an RTI coordinator, the role usually is more limited than that of a reading coach. Most often the RTI coordinator's role includes the following responsibilities:

- Assist the principal with planning RTI implementation
- Train teachers in administering assessments
- Provide refreshers on scoring procedures before each benchmark window
- Consolidate data and provide reports to teachers and the principal

Often RTI coordinators teach intervention groups for a portion of the day and handle coordinator duties the rest of the day. Most often the RTI coordinator is not positioned as an instructional coach as much as most reading coaches. Rarely are RTI coordinators responsible for going into classrooms to observe instruction and providing teachers with structured consultation in how to improve teaching.

BIG QUESTIONS: MONEY, TIME, AND RESULTS

Funding an RTI Initiative

One of the best things about implementing RTI is that, compared with many other initiatives, this one is not expensive. RTI does not require funding to hire new staff or bring in lots of expensive materials. Many schools are successfully implementing RTI by redirecting and focusing the staff that is already in the school and using the instructional materials already there.

The school will need a literacy screening instrument, but most of them are inexpensive. DIBELS is available free online, Virginia's Phonological Awareness and Literacy Screening is available to all Virginia schools, and the Texas Primary Reading Inventory is free to Texas schools and can be purchased at nominal cost for use in other states. The two major expenses include professional development for the teachers and sometimes additional intervention materials or programs. Professional development may help in providing a common understanding about the reasons to implement RTI, the uses of data, and the three-tier reading model approach.

How Long Does It Take to Implement?

It will take 3 years to fully implement RTI and up to 5 years to see the full impact of the new practices on student scores. To a great extent this estimate depends on what other initiatives your staff has implemented, the current approaches to teaching reading, and the knowledge and skills of your teaching staff. If your teachers have strong background knowledge of scientifically based reading research and good reading instructional practices, it may go more quickly.

Teaching a staff to learn how to use data is not the hardest part of an implementation. The hardest part is teaching the staff to improve the quality of instruction and learn how to intensify instruction when student progress is insufficient. One hurdle for the staff to overcome is to view RTI as a framework for decision making and not a model. RTI is a way of thinking about how to organize instruction to respond to student needs based on assessment data. This must be viewed as a change management process, along with the rollout of processes and practices that will be new to your staff.

The term "three-tier reading model" has become very popular. The major contribution it has provided is a schema for thinking about an instructional delivery model. However, it is not a model to be adopted and followed rigidly. It's a mistake to think of RTI as a model to install in a school. RTI is a paradigm and is best implemented in a customized way by the school staff. It's a change process that relies on staff buy-in. Each school implements RTI in a unique manner. Each grade level teacher team needs to figure out how they want to organize and schedule to provide tiers of instruction for their students.

> *As a school enters its second and third years of RTI implementation, the framework is applied in a more fluid manner. Movement of students between levels is more gradual. Knowing how to intensify instruction becomes second nature.*

As a school enters its second and third year of RTI implementation, the framework is applied in a more fluid manner. Movement of students between levels is more gradual. Knowing how to intensify instruction becomes second nature. After the first year, data analysis is no longer occurring just at checkpoint meetings but is part of the intuitive approach to problem solving for students.

What Level of Success Can I Expect?

According to Torgesen (2004, pp. 6–10), research findings show that when reading interventions are early and effective, all but 1–4% of students reach average reading levels. Set your school goal at 95% of K–3 students reading at benchmark. Kindergarten and first grade will achieve success quickest. For middle schools, expect to increase the number of students at benchmark by 10% per year.

Progress is slower at Grades 2 and 3 than in kindergarten and first grade and even slower again at fourth, fifth, and sixth grades. For second and third grade, expect to increase the percentage of students reaching benchmark by at least 20 percentage points the first year of implementation. However, it generally takes 3 years or more to get 80%–90% of third graders to benchmark if your school starts the process with less than 40% reading at grade level. Struggling second- and third-grade readers are missing more skills, and they are further behind. For example, third graders can be struggling on word patterns that are generally mastered in first grade and those their benchmark peers have mastered in second grade. Not only are more skills missing, but it takes longer for students to make progress the later they begin intervention. After your school has implemented RTI for a couple of years, fewer and fewer students will be leaving first grade behind, and so the success is easier to maintain across grade levels.

It is harder to estimate expected levels of success at the middle school level. First, there is less research on implementing RTI for middle schools than for elementary schools. Just like in second and third grades, factors related to students are more complex than in kindergarten and first grade, including a larger number of different skills to be covered in groups and the greater need to use diagnostic assessments to pinpoint deficit skills. Implementing RTI is more challenging in middle school, not only because of student factors but also because the infrastructure issues are more substantive, such as scheduling and teacher knowledge base. For example, a major issue is how to schedule the extensive amount of time a student needs, which may be up to 2 hours of intervention daily. Additionally, some experts advocate that phonics and phonemic awareness skills cannot be bypassed to concentrate only on fluency and comprehension. Teachers need programs and materials to teach skills that many have not had experience teaching.

Delivering Intervention Instruction

I love the small group instruction. I am able to work on the specific skills that my students need. The difference this has made is amazing.

—Interventionist

ORGANIZING FOR INTERVENTION GROUPS

Planning can make the process of launching intervention instruction go more smoothly once the fall data are available. Based on my experience, two factors have a significant impact on how easily RTI can be implemented in a school. The first is how accustomed teachers are to teaching small groups. Teachers who regularly deliver small-group instruction are more comfortable and accomplished in working with one intervention group while the rest of the class works independently at literacy work stations. The second factor is the degree to which the teachers and administrators are familiar with working with student data to inform instruction. If they have already been using formative data to inform instruction and there is a "data culture" in the school, RTI implementation goes more smoothly. If not, then teachers need more time and support to learn to use data and manage small groups.

Some key decisions that can be made during the planning stage are in the area of selecting and organizing the delivery model for small-group intervention instruction for each grade level. This includes deciding who will provide instruction, whether it will take place in the classroom or as a pull-out, and when intervention will occur.

Who Teaches Intervention Groups?

Deciding who will teach the intervention groups is an important strategic decision. Common options are that all intervention groups will be taught by Title I or reading teachers, or the classroom teacher teaches all the small groups, or groups are taught by a combination of both the classroom teacher and support personnel. For a variety of reasons, it is important for the classroom teacher to teach at least some of the groups. This way, the classroom teachers will learn more about data analysis and the unique characteristics of intervention instruction and improve their skills in providing differentiated instruction in the core program. When classroom teachers are interventionists, it also limits the passing of struggling readers to other staff.

> *Learning to provide data-driven intervention instruction in small groups improves a classroom teacher's skills in providing differentiated instruction in the core program.*

If your school has personnel funded through Title I or other sources, RTI is an opportunity to align the staff members who work with struggling readers. In the past there have been too many separate services that weren't well coordinated. Launching RTI provides an opportunity for all staff to use the same screening data to group students and to determine what skills a student lacks. All staff members must be trained together in the use of the data and in the collaborative problem-solving techniques to determine what a student needs, which students he or she will be grouped with, and who will teach them. Classroom teachers need to have collaboration time with the other support staff to talk about the students they have shared responsibility to teach.

When Does Intervention Instruction Take Place?

Principals are key in the dialogue to determine when the intervention groups will occur. Groups can be taught during a scheduled intervention block time or be embedded in the language arts block. I recommend that the principal work with each grade level team to designate a 30-minute intervention block during the day and then, once the decision is made, include it in the master schedule. Adding an intervention block to the master schedule communicates that the principal values this activity (see the sample master schedule in Table 2.1). When the time for intervention is not explicit, it is harder to monitor whether each teacher is actually dedicating 30 minutes daily to intervention groups.

An informational RTI overview meeting should be planned for all district principals before school starts or early in the fall. A second RTI meeting should follow a couple of months later. At the first 2-hour meeting, principals will hear an overview about RTI, along with some data showing what kind of improvements in student scores are possible with full-scale implementation of data-driven intervention instruction in small groups. A second half-day meeting with the principals and literacy coaches should be held in April. This timing for the spring meeting is ideal because principals have finished the state testing and are thinking ahead to next year. Discussions about alternative ways to organize for intervention groups should surface in this meeting, leading principals to add an intervention block to their master schedule and thereby help teachers plan for this priority time.

At some point in the process, district leadership may choose to require intervention blocks to ensure implementation across all buildings. Reading coaches from one district may express concern about the lack of consistency in the implementation of RTI from one school to another. These coaches could perform their jobs better if the leaders at the top took a stand and required that the RTI model include intervention blocks and three tiers of instruction in every school.

Planning time for intervention at the middle school level is much more challenging. The schedule is more rigid, with students traveling between classrooms to receive instruction from more specialized teachers. Experts recommend dedicating 2 hours a day to reading intervention at this age in order to close the gap. One approach is to convert the English period, plus the student's elective, to a reading remediation block. When these two periods are scheduled back to back and the passing period is eliminated, it is possible to get a block of 2 hours. Rather than expecting all teachers to teach intervention groups, it may be better at the middle school level to select a few teachers and train them extensively in reading instruction. Many middle school teachers do not have the background in instructional techniques for working with struggling readers, especially those whose deficits require instruction in reading skills more typically taught in first through third grade.

Where Does Intervention Occur?

Intervention groups can be taught in a number of locations, including inside or outside the general education classroom. No research supports one approach as necessarily better than another. A number of factors may be relevant in considering where the groups should be taught. When the instruction occurs in the general education classroom, teachers can use the classroom management procedures they have already established for center time to ease into scheduling intervention group time.

However, one critical difference is that instead of the teacher walking around supervising students working at the independent centers, the teacher will be at a teaching table providing direct instruction to one intervention group.

If there is a support teacher who can assist with groups, one approach is for the support teacher to come into the classroom at a specified time daily. When the interventionist arrives, the teacher will teach one intervention group in one corner, the interventionist will teach a second group in another corner, and the benchmark students will work at independent work stations. There is less loss of time because the students don't leave the classroom and travel to another location. Having the interventionist in the classroom with the teacher may also facilitate communication between the two teachers.

When a support teacher pushes into the classroom to teach intervention groups at the same time that the classroom teacher instructs a group, these two teachers are working with 6–10 students, leaving fewer students working independently at literacy work stations. This also helps the teacher because two groups are seen at the same time. He or she might have a third group to schedule at another time. When a classroom teacher and another teacher are both interventionists, the classroom may be arranged as shown in Figure 3.1.

Figure 3.1   Delivery Model With Teacher and Push-In Interventionist

Push-In Intervention Support

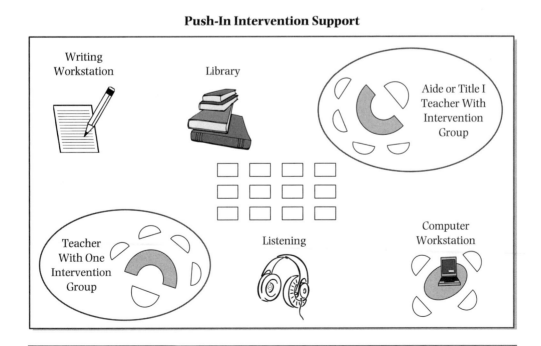

There are other considerations for where the small groups are taught. Sometimes groups are pulled outside the classroom so the teacher can more easily hear the students in the small group (Figure 3.2). Also, pulling a group out sometimes enables students to focus better, without the distraction of what the other students are doing.

Figure 3.2   Delivery Model With Teacher and Pull-Out Interventionist

Pull-Out Intervention Support

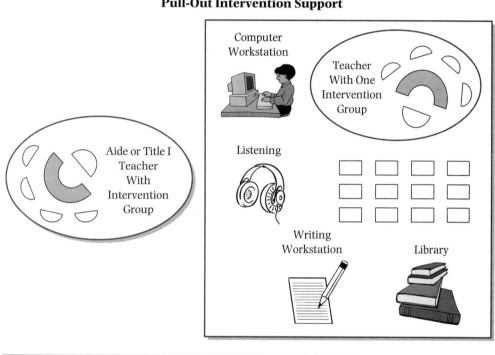

Another delivery model that has been especially popular at second grade and above can be called the walk-to-intervention model because students walk to the location where they will receive their intervention group instruction (Figure 3.3). This model requires that all teachers at a grade level schedule intervention at the same time so that they can group across the classrooms. Availability of other support personnel during this intervention block is critical so that some of the groups can be as small as three students. Some of the advantages of this model are that every group is led by a teacher, students are not missing another activity to participate in the intervention group, and teachers can specialize in a particular area and use special materials. This model is particularly useful for higher grade levels because there are too many skill areas that students may need, making it nearly impossible for a classroom teacher to meet with all the groups. Teachers who use guided reading groups during their English language arts (ELA) block like this approach because it means that they don't have to plan additional time when some students are working independently. Sometimes two teachers trade students during intervention time rather than grouping across the entire grade level (Figure 3.4).

Figure 3.3   Walk-to-Intervention Delivery Model

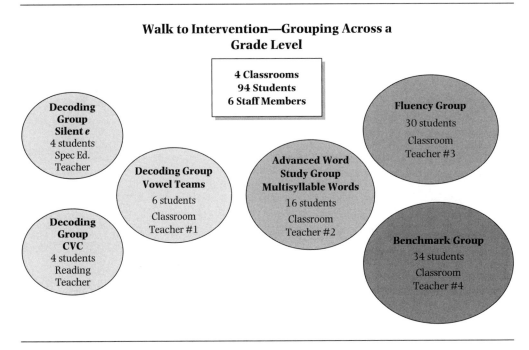

Walk to Intervention—Grouping Across a Grade Level

4 Classrooms
94 Students
6 Staff Members

Decoding Group Silent *e*
4 students
Spec Ed. Teacher

Decoding Group CVC
4 students
Reading Teacher

Decoding Group Vowel Teams
6 students
Classroom Teacher #1

Advanced Word Study Group Multisyllable Words
16 students
Classroom Teacher #2

Fluency Group
30 students
Classroom Teacher #3

Benchmark Group
34 students
Classroom Teacher #4

Figure 3.4   Partial Walk-to Delivery Model

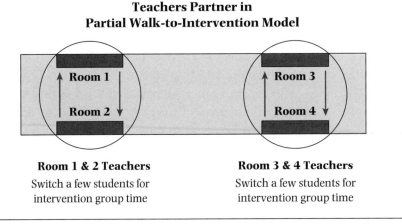

Teachers Partner in Partial Walk-to-Intervention Model

Room 1
Room 2

Room 3
Room 4

Room 1 & 2 Teachers
Switch a few students for intervention group time

Room 3 & 4 Teachers
Switch a few students for intervention group time

TIERS OF INTERVENTION INSTRUCTION

One of the important foundations of the RTI model is that tiers of instruction are available to meet the needs of each student. Although there could be any number of tiers, the use of three tiers became popular with the publication of *Introduction to the 3-Tier Reading Model* by the Vaughn Gross Center for Reading and Language Arts in 2005. This center is directed by Dr. Sharon Vaughn, one of the leading researchers in the field of early reading intervention.

The term *framework* may be preferable because *model* sounds too much like a set approach. One of the best things about the three-tier framework is that it is useful in establishing a common set of terms to use in talking about layers of instruction and students moving from one layer to another.

Tier I

Tier I is generally viewed as the ELA instruction students receive in the general education classroom. This instruction, typically scheduled as a 90- to 120-minute block that is often uninterrupted, includes all five essential components of reading instruction. That means that the curriculum includes instruction in phonemic awareness, phonics, fluency, vocabulary, and comprehension to varying degrees, depending on the grade level. Oral language and writing are also important. Many schools use a research-based, purchased curriculum for their ELA block, sometimes called a basal. One reason many districts choose to adopt a purchased curriculum is that developing a curriculum for K–3 reading, and all the accompanying materials, is complex and time consuming. In order to write the curriculum, teachers would need to know how to develop lessons that teach skills using an explicit, systematic, and sequential approach. Although it is possible for teachers to design curricula in many areas, designing effective curriculum for early reading is complex because of the sequential nature of the skills and the difficulty of integrating the five essential components.

Intervention groups are homogeneous by skill deficit and typically are smaller and more focused than small groups during the core time.

The ELA block often is called the core reading instruction. Regardless of whether a purchased program is used or the school uses a teacher-designed curriculum, it is typically delivered in multiple grouping formats. Good practice is to plan a combination of whole class and small-group instruction. Small groups during the core time are not the same as small groups for intervention instruction for struggling readers. During the ELA block students often are grouped heterogeneously.

Intervention groups are homogeneous by skill deficit and typically are smaller and more focused than small groups during the core time.

Assessments to measure the effectiveness of the Tier I instruction include the end-of-unit tests included in the basal and the universal screening typically administered three times per year to ensure that all students are making adequate progress to maintain their benchmark status. Ongoing benchmark assessments with a screening instrument that is nationally normed (and not produced by the basal publisher) are critical. This ensures that the Tier I instruction is of high quality and effective, keeping a majority of students at the benchmark level with core instruction alone. Experts suggest that 70%–80% of students should achieve benchmark levels with Tier I alone. Although it is possible to compensate for weaknesses of the Tier I curriculum by placing students in intervention groups, serving too many students will overtax the Tier II and Tier III system.

Tier II

Tier II can be considered the first line of intervention for students who are not at benchmark with the core instruction. Tier II is not provided to all students. It is only for those who need it, based on their below-benchmark scores on an early literacy screening. It is also not designed to last forever; it is intentionally designed to be short term. Tier II intervention instruction is very focused and covers only targeted skill areas. In most schools, Tier II instruction occurs at a time outside the ELA block so that the below-benchmark students do not miss some Tier I instruction for intervention. The curriculum for Tier II can be either lessons that the teacher designs or lessons outlined in a purchased program. In many schools, the classroom teacher teaches Tier II intervention groups. In other schools, support personnel serve as interventionists, including Title I teachers, reading specialists, and instructional aides. Instruction may take place in the general education classroom or a quieter location.

Intervention groups are formed homogeneously by skill needs. Students who are below benchmark and need more help are placed together in homogeneous groups based on skill deficits. These skill groups are *not* ability groups. During a recent RTI workshop for a large group of educators, one teacher raised a concern about whether grouping homogeneously is appropriate. She asserted that the reading field had moved away from the "robin" and "bluebird" groups of the past, which were names that teachers gave groups in order to disguise from students their placement in a high or low reading group. There are many benefits of students participating in heterogeneous groups for much of their reading instruction, especially for comprehension discussions about a story read aloud and dialogue about new vocabulary words. Yet intervention groups must be homogeneous in order to be effective. Keep in mind that intervention groups meet for only a short part of the day and do not make up the student's entire reading instruction. An additional consideration is that assignment to homogeneous intervention groups is temporary because the groups are flexible, unlike reading groups of the past that often remained intact for the entire academic year.

The instruction in Tier II is teacher directed; peers working together or students working independently in centers do not qualify as Tier II instruction. Students who are not mastering early literacy skills through the Tier I core instruction need time with a teacher who can reteach a skill, followed by time for the student to practice and receive immediate corrective feedback. Only through the careful guidance of a teacher will the student get a chance to correct his or her misunderstandings and slowly gain mastery and confidence. This type of explicit instruction with guided feedback is the work of a skilled teacher and cannot be duplicated by a peer or in an unsupervised setting such as a computer station.

Some teachers have the knowledge and skills to design effective intervention lessons, and others do not. Schools need to decide whether to purchase intervention programs for use in the Tier II groups, and then which groups should be placed in these programs. If teachers with less foundational knowledge about reading instruction or fewer skills in guided error correction procedures will be instructing the groups, it is wise for the school to purchase more structured materials and programs for these teachers. To ensure the best solution for a school, often a combination of purchased programs and teacher-designed lessons is optimal.

> Only through the careful guidance of a teacher will the student get a chance to correct his or her misunderstandings and slowly gain mastery and confidence. This type of explicit instruction with guided feedback is the work of a skilled teacher and cannot be duplicated by a peer or in an unsupervised setting such as a computer station.

Intervention programs are needed for the most challenging students and for the most structured areas of instruction. For example, it makes sense to purchase materials for phonics and fluency and then provide teachers with training in how to design lessons for phonemic awareness, vocabulary, and comprehension. The school may elect to purchase a structured program that combines several of these areas of instruction for the lowest-scoring students. There are many excellent programs that provide structured lesson plans that include phonemic awareness, letter recognition, and basic phonics. Students need to remain in the ELA block for instruction in vocabulary and comprehension if these components are not the focus of the intervention group.

The effectiveness of Tier II instruction is measured by periodic progress monitoring of the students in intervention groups. Progress monitoring is essential for intervention students and not necessary for benchmark students unless the data indicate that they are at risk of slipping. Most schools assess students receiving Tier II intervention every 2 or 3 weeks. Decisions about how often to progress monitor must balance the benefits of obtaining more data points (which increases confidence in a trend line) with the detriment of using valuable instructional time to administer assessments. My recommendation is to assess only as often as teachers can really use the data; however, standard practice is to monitor at least monthly. It is critical to have at least three data points before concluding that a student's rate of progress supports continued participation in the group or movement to another group. It is common for schools to assess less frequently when they first implement RTI and increase the frequency after the teachers have received adequate training in how to use the data to inform decisions.

Tier III

Tier III instruction is designed for students whose progress in Tier II has been insufficient. In most schools, Tier III is not special education but is more intensive intervention to try to improve the progress and avoid the necessity of placement in special education. Most of the time students are placed in a Tier II group first and then moved to Tier III only if the rate of progress is inadequate. However, some students are placed in Tier III immediately, based on evidence that the level of intensity in Tier II will not be adequate.

The Tier III student is more likely to be behind in many skill areas, not just with a few gaps, like the more typical Tier II student. For example, in the middle of kindergarten a student is well below benchmark in letter naming and phonological awareness, as measured by Letter Naming Fluency (LNF), Initial Sound Fluency (ISF), and Phoneme Segmentation Fluency (PSF) in Dynamic Indicators of Basic Early Literacy Skills (DIBELS). The student is also not making connections between letters and sounds, as measured by Nonsense Word Fluency (NWF) in DIBELS. The student has been in a Tier II group since the beginning of the year and has not made much gain in scores despite excellent instruction daily in a group of three or four students. The other three students in the same group have made tremendous progress.

Tier III is different from Tier II in a number of critical ways. Students in Tier III generally need more time in intervention groups to make progress. The instruction is characterized by extraordinary intensity and focus. Tier III instruction is even more systematic and is slower paced, with more practice cycles for a given concept.

Often the curriculum in Tier III is different. Whereas a teacher-designed lesson plan may work for the students with gaps in Tier II, students in Tier III generally need a program in which the skills are arranged in a sequence. Because the student is missing so many concepts, all skills are taught rather than just a few. Many schools use a program for Tier III, but it is also important that instruction is provided by a skilled teacher who can individualize within the program. In some cases it could be the same curriculum as used in Tier II but intensified in frequency, duration, and practice cycles. It is also taught from beginning to end, whereas in Tier II the teacher may skip around and teach only missing skills.

One of the most important characteristics of Tier III instruction is that it is more intensive than Tier II. What makes instruction more intensive? Often intensity is in the way a concept is taught. When a skill is first presented, the teacher uses more modeling to show the task, and she provides more scaffolding to help the student be successful. The teacher may break the task down into smaller parts and use a graphic organizer or manipulatives for each part. The teacher may modify the modes of task presentation to help the student understand or increase the structure of the task to make all the steps more explicit. Providing more repetition cycles and more corrective feedback can intensify instruction. Increasing the amount and types of cues and prompts also helps. The teacher will gradually remove scaffolding until the student can demonstrate mastery.

Also constituting more intensive instruction are the personalized attention possible in working with a very small group of students; the fast-paced interaction between the student and teacher, where the student is actively engaged in thinking and responding many times every minute; and the more open-ended questions that require a response beyond a simple yes or no answer.

In *Introduction to the 3-Tier Reading Model* (Vaughn Gross Center for Reading and Language Arts, 2005), 60 minutes of additional intervention time is recommended for Tier III students. This is twice as much intervention time as for Tier II instruction and is assumed to be above and beyond the Tier I ELA block. Because these students are further behind, it's impossible to accelerate their progress and catch them up with less or equal instructional time.

The assessments for Tier III include progress monitoring every week or two and use of additional informal diagnostic assessments such as phonological and phonics screening instruments to pinpoint skill deficits. Some of these informal diagnostic screening instruments provide alternative forms for progress monitoring to confirm that a student has mastered one skill before moving him or her to the next skill in sequence.

PROCESSES FOR MOVING STUDENTS THROUGH THE SYSTEM

One of the most challenging practices for schools is establishing the decision-making processes that will determine placement of students in groups and their movement from Tier II to Tier III. In many publications about RTI, two alternative models for decision making are described. These models represent different approaches to placing students in intervention instruction and moving them between tiers. The two models are the protocol model and the problem-solving model. Each is described in this section, along with guidance about which approach most schools use.

Protocol Model Versus Problem-Solving Model

The protocol model focuses on the use of a protocol for instruction, or a prescribed intervention curriculum. The school or district selects a single intervention curriculum, and all below-benchmark students at a grade level are placed in groups to receive the same intervention. Embedded in the protocol model is a belief that the right program will improve the skills of all (or enough) students.

The problem-solving model is an approach whereby decisions about what the student needs are made on a student-by-student basis. Not every child gets the same thing because they don't all have the same deficits. Based on data, a teacher or team makes decisions about what to provide students (Table 3.1).

Many schools use a combination of these two approaches. One possible combination of approaches is that a school determines a selection of intervention programs or materials and then uses a problem-solving approach to place students in these intervention alternatives. This model acknowledges that one intervention will not efficiently meet the needs of all struggling readers yet limits the number of possible interventions so that it is easier to train staff and track results.

My recommendation is to implement the problem-solving model because it encourages decisions about how to differentiate instruction based on deficit skills and, in my experience, produces better results for students. The school can establish a toolkit of intervention programs or curricula, and teachers can select from among these choices. In the protocol model, not enough students make substantial gains in reading scores with a single approach to providing intervention. Additionally, teachers need to learn to analyze the assessment data and use them to inform their decisions, and the problem-solving model supports that process. The problem-solving model takes more time and analysis, but the results for students make it worth the effort.

Table 3.1   Comparison of the Protocol and Problem-Solving Models

	Advantages	Disadvantages
Protocol model	No time spent in making decisions about students.	May lead to lack of buy-in from teachers because teacher input about individual students is not included.
	Staff trained in one intervention curriculum instead of many.	Presumes that the program is the key to student success.
	No need for data analysis on student needs if one program (limited need if multiple programs).	Loss of opportunity to teach staff to analyze data from screening and diagnostic data.
	Easier to evaluate the effectiveness of the intervention because all students receive the same instruction.	Discourages differentiation of delivery to meet individual student needs.
Problem-solving model	Presumes that the teacher's instruction is the main ingredient for success instead of a program.	Staff must be knowledgeable and well trained.
	Key assumption that one size doesn't fit all students.	Time and processes are needed for staff to analyze data and determine instruction for each student.
	Relies heavily on data.	Requires structured data collection and management techniques and staff ability to effectively interpret data.
	Use of many alternative approaches enables a more customized approach for each student.	School has to deal with complexity of making decisions using multiple data sources and alternative programs or strategies for instruction.
	Groups and instruction are flexible.	Evaluation of specific program effectiveness is more difficult.

Placing Students in Intervention

It helps to have an explicit process, understood by all school staff, for making decisions about placing students in groups and moving them between groups. One indication of the degree of implementation is to ask teachers to describe how placement decisions are made. Who is involved in the initial placement decision? Which data are examined? How often are the data graphed and examined? How can the staff tell whether a student is making an adequate rate of progress? What happens if the student's progress is insufficient?

In Reading First schools, often the reading coach and teacher meet individually to determine group placement for each below-benchmark student. The principal may be involved in these meetings, although most of the time the coach shares the final grouping with the principal after the teacher meetings occur. Many coaches prefer to meet individually with the teachers rather than in grade-level meetings. Some teachers are more comfortable sharing confidential information about students in this setting. Many schools schedule these data analysis consultations the week after completion of the fall and winter benchmark assessments. These benchmarks provide checkpoint times when it is helpful to discuss progress of all the students in a teacher's class. By the second year of RTI implementation, most schools have more informal and frequent data discussions. The process becomes more fluid as time goes on.

Making Group Placement Decisions

If the grade-level team has selected the walk-to-intervention model, where there is an established intervention block and students receive intervention from teachers other than their homeroom teachers, then grouping decisions typically are made at a grade-level team meeting rather than in one-on-one meetings with a reading coach. All the teachers at a grade level are involved. The team has to determine which skill groups are needed, who will teach each group, where the groups will meet, and which students will be placed in each group. The walk-to-intervention model is the most popular delivery model with teachers in second grade and beyond. Yet because it is the most collaborative model, the team of teachers must work well together for it to be successful. If teachers don't trust their colleagues to teach their students well, the process breaks down.

Placement of students in groups for the walk-to-intervention model can be done at one 45-minute grade-level team meeting if each teacher comes to the meeting prepared. Before the meeting, each teacher needs to analyze the errors of all below-benchmark students in his or her class to identify which skills are lacking and where on the skill continuum to start intervention instruction. Below-benchmark students are placed in groups for comprehension only, fluency only, or one of several phonics groups. When the skill deficit is phonics, the teacher needs to decide which type of word pattern the student needs first. Labels can be placed on the table indicating each specific skill area, and then each teacher walks around the table and places his or her student booklets on the appropriate pile to place a student in the group working on that skill. The piles show the number of students in each skill group, and then staffing can be allocated according to guidelines for recommended group sizes.

Allocation of staffing is important to keep the groups as small as possible, especially for the students at the lowest skill areas. Other than the benchmark and fluency groups, the ideal group size is no more than five students, with the lowest groups capped at three. An example of the groups for one third-grade team follows. In this example, there are 85 students in four third-grade classrooms, and four extra support staff members are assigned to teach groups at the designated intervention block time. The eight groups might look like this:

- 30 students at benchmark, taught by classroom teacher #1
- 23 below-benchmark students who need only fluency improvement, taught by classroom teacher #2
- 12 students in a group for multisyllable words, taught by a reading specialist
- 5 students in a group for *r*-controlled vowels, taught by a Title I teacher
- 5 students in a group for long vowel teams, taught by classroom teacher #3
- 4 students in a group for the long vowel silent *e* pattern, taught by a Title I teacher
- 3 students in a group for short vowels, taught by a reading specialist
- 3 students in a group for short vowels, taught by classroom teacher #4

When the grade-level meeting is completed, each teacher knows what group she will teach and where the below-benchmark students in her classroom are placed.

Grouping Techniques

Grouping is one of the most difficult analytical processes because it has to be completed at the outset. To launch RTI, teachers will need help from an expert the first time through. One of the most critical concepts for teachers to understand is that they cannot group by the instructional recommendation level alone. The student's instructional recommendation level (benchmark, strategic, or intensive) tells *who*, not *what*; an instructional level tells which students need intervention but not enough about what type of instruction is needed. The levels can be an indicator of the degree of urgency because the intensive students generally are low in all the indicators measured at that time. Although grouping by instructional

> *The student's instructional recommendation level (benchmark, strategic, or intensive) tells who, not what; an instructional level tells which students need intervention but not enough about what type of instruction is needed.*

recommendation levels might work for the intensive students because they generally are below benchmark in all the skills measured, it doesn't work well for the strategic students because they often are not low in the same skills.

Because grouping by instructional recommendation level is not recommended, what approaches are better? One simple way to group is by the skills on which the student scores below benchmark. Although this is better than grouping by instructional recommendation level, it is still a fairly basic approach. The best approach to grouping is to examine whether the student has problems with accuracy or fluency and to identify exact skill deficits when the issue is accuracy.

In order to demonstrate to teachers that they need to dig deeper than the score, the scoring probes in Table 3.2 from two different first-grade students are helpful.

Table 3.2   Two First-Grade Students With the Same Score and Different Needs

What Does This Student Need?
NWF Example

k̸ i k	w ø j	s̸ i g	f a j	y̸ i s	11/15
k̸ a̸ j	f̸ e̸ k	a v	z̸ i n	z e z	9/14
l a n	n̸ u l	z e m̸	o̸ g	n o m̸	10/14
y̸ u̸ f	p̸ o s	v ø k	v i v	f e g̸	9/15
b̸ u̸ b̸	d̸ i j	s i j	v u s	t o s	1/15

Total = 40

Same Score—Same Level
NWF Example

k i k	w o j	s i g	f a j	y i s	15/15
k a y̸	f̸ e̸ k	a v	z i n	z e̸ z	11/14
l a n	n u̸ l	z e̸ m	o g	n o m	12/14
y u̸ f	p o s	v o k	v i v	f e g	2/15
b u b	d i j	s i j	v u s	t o s	__/15

Total = 40

These two first-grade students both have an NWF score of 40. The first student is reading sound by sound and not blending at all (as revealed by the lines under each letter) and is missing both consonants and vowels. The second student is reading the words blended (as indicated by a single line under all the letters in a nonsense word) and is missing only the vowels *e* and *u*. Although they both have a score of 40, these two students do not need the same instruction, and placement of the second student in the group with the first one will slow down this child's progress.

The same point is demonstrated in Table 3.3 with two third-grade students.

Table 3.3   Two Third-Grade Students With the Same Score and Different Needs

---

Third Grade: Score is 82 wpm

Benchmark I. I DIBELS™ Oral Reading Fluency

My Friend

I have a new friend at school. She can't walk so she uses a	14
wheelchair to get around. She comes to school in a special van	26
that can transport four people who use wheelchairs. The van	36
brings my friend and another boy to school. My friend is in third	49
grade with me, and the boy is a fourth grader.	59
I like to watch my friend get in and out of the van. The driver	74
pushes a button and part of the van floor lowers to the driveway	87
to form a ramp. My friend just wheels up the ramp and goes	100
inside. After she is inside, the driver pushes the button and the	112
ramp puts itself away. When it is time to get out of the van, they	127
do the same thing again. Sometimes I help open the door so she	140

82/108 = 76% Accuracy

Third Grade: Score is 82 wpm

Benchmark I. I DIBELS™ Oral Reading Fluency

My Friend

I have a new friend at school. She can't walk so she uses a	14
wheelchair to get around. She comes to school in a special van	26
that can transport four people who use wheelchairs. The van	36
brings my friend and another boy to school. My friend is in third	49
grade with me, and the boy is a fourth grader.	59
I like to watch my friend get in and out of the van. The driver	74
pushes a button and part of the van floor lowers to the driveway	87
to form a ramp. My friend just wheels up the ramp and goes	100
inside. After she is inside, the driver pushes the button and the	112
ramp puts itself away. When it is time to get out of the van, they	127
do the same thing again. Sometimes I help open the door so she	140

82/83 = 99% Accuracy

Although they both have a score of 82 on Oral Reading Fluency (ORF), the first student read 108 words and got 26 words wrong, resulting in an accuracy rate of 76%. The second student read all but one word correctly but didn't get very far in the passage for a minute, indicating a fluency issue. After a review of the patterns of errors for the first student, an informal phonics screening would be needed to confirm the skill deficit areas for intervention.

Early literacy screening tools assess the subskills of early reading in kindergarten and first grade, whereas the most critical indicator for second grade and above is the student's ability to read a minimum level of words correctly in a grade-level passage. As an example, the DIBELS measures letter naming, phonemic awareness, and the alphabetic principle in kindergarten and first grade. The LNF score in kindergarten and throughout first grade measures the student's ability to recognize and name letters. Experts debate about whether letter naming is needed for reading. Even if letter naming is not a reading skill, measuring LNF is a robust predictor of later success, possibly because it serves as a proxy for parental involvement in the learning-to-read process or the level of a student's preschool preparation. ISF and PSF measure phonemic awareness, critical early literacy skills. NWF measures two skills: knowledge of letter-sound correspondences and ability to blend sounds into words. In the middle of first grade, ORF is measured and serves as an indication of the student's acquisition of sight words and ability to read consonant-vowel-consonant words in text. Deficits in any of the kindergarten and first grade indicators can be used for grouping because the subskills that are measured must be developed for good reading.

In second and third grade, ORF is the primary curriculum-based measure, assessing the student's overall level of success in reading a minimum number of words correctly per minute in a grade-level passage. The student must decode words accurately and with enough fluency to make it through enough words in a minute to achieve a benchmark score. If the student cannot read correctly the benchmark number of words in a minute, the student probe reveals whether the problem is accuracy, fluency, or both. If there are few words slashed, then the student would benefit from instruction to increase his or her ability to read passages more fluently. If a great number of words are read incorrectly, the process is more involved. For any student who reads less than 95% of the words correctly, the next step is to analyze the errors to explore which word patterns are difficult for the student. This can serve as a hypothesis, but use of a phonics screening tool to confirm the word pattern difficulties is essential because many words contain several word patterns. For example, if the student misses the word *elderly*, the problematic word pattern could be the ending *-ly*, the *r*-control vowel pattern, or some other part of the word.

The only way to know for sure is to use a phonics screener that assesses each isolated word pattern skill.

The tightest grouping occurs when students are placed in groups by the skill deficit areas and not the range of scores on curriculum-based measures (CBMs). For example, instead of placing together third-grade students who scored below 60 words correct in a minute, a careful analysis of whether the problem is fluency or accuracy is needed. If the problem is accuracy, scores on the skills of a phonics screener can be summarized on a chart. Groups then can be formed by skill deficit areas. An example is provided in Table 3.4.

Table 3.4   Group Placement Using Data From *Phonics Screener for Intervention*™

Grouping Sample Third-Grade Class

Student Name	1a: Letter Names	1b: Letter Sounds	2: VC/CVC	3: Consonant Blends	4: Consonant Digraphs	5: Silent -e	6: Vowel Teams (Predictable)	7: Vowel Teams	8: Vowel -r	9: Complex Consonants	Sight Words
			Beginning Phonics Skills				Advanced Phonics Skills				Other
Maximum Points	26	21C/ 5V	10/10	10/10	10/10	10/10	10/10	10/10	10/10	10/10	/220
Hilary			6/10	5/10	5/9	8/10					
Anthony			5/10	4/10	6/9	3/9					
Sophie			5/10	2/8	6/10	1/10					
Chaz			8/10	8/9	7/8	8/10					
Brian			7/10	9/10	7/10	9/9					
Tyler			9/10	10/10	8/10	10/10	10/9	9/9	10/10	8/10	
Carlie			8/10	10/9	8/9	8/9	8/8	8/9			
Chandler			6/9	6/10	7/9	7/8					
Taylor			10/10	9/9	9/10	10/10	8/10	7/10	10/8	6/10	

95%
GROUP INC

As teachers learn to interpret data for grouping students by skill deficit areas and to plan appropriate intervention instruction, one of their most powerful aids is the use of a continuum of skills. Both phonological awareness and phonics encompass a series of skills that can be arranged from easiest to hardest. For example, in phonological awareness students generally become aware of syllables before individual sounds in words. Also, the ability to isolate a single sound in a word (usually the first, last, and then middle) precedes segmenting and blending all the sounds. Phoneme segmentation is necessary before phoneme substitution, the skill used when a student can change the /s/ sound at the end of the word *bus* to make the word *bug*.

Using one continuum for phonological awareness skills and another continuum for phonics skills helps teachers decide where to start instruction and how to move a student up a level as he or she masters each skill. Additionally, the continuum helps in organizing instructional activities. Teachers create plastic tubs, file boxes, or notebooks to organize activities they use to help students practice the skill in intervention group time.

> *Using one continuum for phonological awareness skills and another continuum for phonics skills helps teachers decide where to start instruction and how to move a student up a level as he or she masters each skill.*

Simplifying the Process

Avoid making the process too complex at first. If the teachers are spending too much time moving students between groups, this extensive planning time usually is at the expense of instructional time. It is best for the coach to become an expert at data analysis and grouping and to play an integral role in helping the teachers group their students, especially at first. Over time the teachers can be given more responsibility for grouping as they become more and more familiar with the process.

Avoid regrouping too often. Sometimes an RTI coordinator or reading coach begins to understand what the data mean and wants to regroup every couple of weeks. Although the data are sensitive, and it's possible to measure small changes in student skills, regrouping too often is very frustrating to the teachers. A reasonable balance is to wait for about 8 or 9 weeks before a major regrouping. Most schools form their groups in September, within a week of the end of the fall benchmark assessment period. After some small shifts that first week, these groups typically meet until at least Halloween. They might shift a few students between groups and then continue until the winter holiday. Then the winter benchmark typically is completed just after the students return in January.

Regrouping with the fresh winter benchmark data makes sense. Then these groups can continue until around spring break.

One helpful framework is for the grade-level team to think about the group structure as constant and to move students up in groups as they have mastered the skills in one area and are ready for the next skill in a continuum. This approach is helpful because even if a couple of students move between groups, the entire system isn't disrupted. RTI is based on flexible groups, so it's important to use the progress monitoring data to move students up when they are ready. The school needs to find an appropriate balance between regrouping too often and not often enough.

Another way to simplify the process initially is to narrow the range of strategies and materials for the first 10 weeks of intervention group instruction. Teachers often are overwhelmed if they feel that they need to make a lot of new materials and spend hours organizing them just to start teaching their groups. It is helpful to provide the teachers with lesson plans and about 8–10 activities to teach the first 2–3 weeks of their intervention groups. Then they can meet again as a grade-level team to discuss which instructional strategies are most successful with their students. Many times grade-level teams share lesson plans and share the burden of preparing materials. For example, if at the beginning the principal purchases a copy of the same phonological awareness activity book for each kindergarten teacher, all teachers have access to a common set of activities. To get the process started, the RTI coordinator can select and provide each teacher with materials for about 10 activities from this book. After about 3 weeks, the kindergarten teachers can meet and decide what else they need for the next month. Each teacher can select two activities and prepare duplicate sets of materials for all other teachers. Then when they trade sets, they each will have 6–10 more activities prepared to add to their original set of 10. Another advantage is that they can more effectively share lesson plans.

No time should be lost in initiating intervention groups at the beginning of the year. The week after the end of the benchmark window can be designated for analysis and grouping. The goal is to spend 1 week analyzing the data and placing students into groups so that intervention instruction can start the Monday of the week after the data analysis week. Budgeting funds for a few rotating substitute teachers and releasing classroom teachers for data analysis and grouping are even more important than providing release time to complete the assessments.

Using Progress Monitoring Data

Deficiencies in phonemic awareness and phonics need to be addressed before they can be fluent third-grade readers. RTI gives the students who need instruction the extra help they need.

—Third-grade teacher

Progress monitoring sometimes is the forgotten cousin of benchmark screening. Yet it is the most important part of the RTI process. Progress monitoring is collecting data on at least one of the indicators given in the benchmark periods yet with alternative forms so students cannot remember the prompts or passages. The problem is that after all the effort is expended to complete the benchmark assessments and launch the initial intervention groups, teachers often believe they have no time left to consider collecting and using progress monitoring data.

IMPORTANCE OF PROGRESS MONITORING DATA

Why is progress monitoring so important? It is the heart of RTI. These are the data that are used to make adjustments in instruction along the way. The progress monitoring data allow the principal, RTI coordinator, and teachers to see what is working and what must be changed. They are the data that tell you how well the student is responding to intervention. Not only do they tell you whether instruction is successful for an individual student, they are a check on the effectiveness of the tiers of instruction for a grade level.

> Why is progress monitoring so important? It is the heart of RTI. These are the data that are used to make adjustments in instruction along the way.

Producing and using progress monitoring data is one of the most important components of RTI, yet it is often the first thing principals let go when the teachers begin to talk about being overwhelmed. The progress monitoring data gathered in October, November, and December are needed to motivate the teachers to continue their intervention group time.

When teachers begin to complain that they are overwhelmed with the extra work of organizing to teach these intervention groups, it is tempting to give up the progress monitoring assessments with the idea that there will be data available once the winter benchmark is completed in January. In kindergarten and first grade, the progress monitoring data will show student improvement by November if the teachers have grouped the students tightly, selected materials or strategies that enable them to teach the skill deficits for each group, and have consistently taught the intervention groups. Progress monitoring is exactly what is needed to demonstrate to teachers that RTI is working.

> Progress monitoring is exactly what is needed to demonstrate to teachers that RTI is working, and it's nearly always the first thing a principal gives up when teachers feel overwhelmed.

It is far better to reduce the frequency of progress monitoring than to give it up altogether. For example, if the teachers are feeling overwhelmed the first several months, progress monitoring can be cut back to monthly instead of every 2 weeks. We do not recommend progress monitoring weekly during the first year of RTI implementation because it's too easy for teachers to criticize the extensive amount of time spent assessing. The staff's understanding of how to use the data is more limited at the beginning of the RTI process, so it is easier to justify having a little less data the first year.

After intervention groups are formed and instruction has started, the RTI coordinator can focus on collecting and planning for the use of progress monitoring data. Most principals establish an assessment calendar before the year begins so all teachers know that giving progress monitoring assessments is expected.

DETERMINING WHICH INDICATORS TO PROGRESS MONITOR

It is not necessary to progress monitor all the indicators that are collected at the benchmark periods. Select one or two indicators that measure the skills that are the focus of the instruction for each intervention group and progress monitor only on that indicator or indicators for now. For example, imagine a first-grade group at the middle of the year that did not reach the Dynamic Indicators of Basic Early Literacy Skills (DIBELS) benchmark on either Nonsense Word Fluency (NWF) or Oral Reading Fluency (ORF). If the instructional focus of the group is on teaching the alphabetic principle using words that have the consonant–vowel–consonant (CVC) word pattern, the NWF indicator is a more targeted measure of this skill than the ORF. The first-grade ORF passages contain not only words with the CVC pattern but also nonphonetic sight words and words with other patterns such as words with a long vowel, silent *e* pattern. Although it's a good idea to measure ORF maybe once every 4–6 weeks, progress monitoring with the NWF indicator measures when students have mastered the CVC skill and are ready to move on to other word patterns.

In kindergarten and first grade, DIBELS measures subskills of reading such as phonemic awareness (Initial Sound Fluency [ISF] and Phoneme Segmentation Fluency [PSF]) and the alphabetic principle (NWF). Not only are the skills finite, but the measures are sensitive enough to capture small increases in a student's skills after instruction. Therefore, DIBELS measures are useful for progress monitoring in kindergarten and first grade.

Sometimes it is preferable to progress monitor with a measure other than DIBELS or your selected curriculum-based measure (CBM) assessment, especially at the later grade levels. Teachers who are working with an intervention group of students in second grade and beyond, in which the students are reading well below grade level, will not get much information by progress monitoring with the grade-level ORF if the student is reading inaccurately. Progress monitoring with the informal phonics screener provides more useful data than using ORF if the students are receiving intervention in phonics and word study skills. Progress monitoring with an alternative form of the phonics screener reveals when to move the student up to the next group on the phonics continuum. Teachers can progress monitor with ORF periodically, but less frequently, until the student has mastered the types of word patterns expected for a student of his or her grade level.

If students read at least 95% of the words in the passage accurately but are not at benchmark because of poor fluency, then they do not need intervention in phonics and word study. They need instruction, guided practice, and independent practice in reading more fluently at the passage level. Progress monitoring with CBM oral reading passages is very helpful in tracking the rate of progress for the students receiving fluency intervention.

GRAPHING RATES OF PROGRESS

Graphing progress monitoring data is one of the most important ways to use the data. From the point when a student first enters intervention, a graph is prepared and the teacher draws a targetline from the student's initial data point to the expected level of performance. This line shows the teacher the level of growth the student needs to achieve to reach benchmark. This required rate of progress for the student is a constant reminder that the goal is to close the gap and reach benchmark rather than to be satisfied with some progress in the current year.

The progress monitoring targetline graph helps in comparing actual with expected level of progress. Every time the teacher administers a progress monitoring assessment, the new point is added to this graph. Once a minimum of three progress monitoring points have been collected for a student, the teacher can compare the actual data points with the targetline. All data points that fall below the targetline reveal inadequate progress. Comparing the actual with expected performance is critical for determining whether the rate of progress is sufficient.

Principals need these progress monitoring graphs for a number of reasons. The first is to determine whether the delivery model selected by a grade level is effective. This can be assessed at a grade level meeting where each teacher sorts his or her progress monitoring graphs into two piles; one pile includes students progressing above the targetline, and the second pile includes those whose progress monitoring points fall below the targetline. If the majority of the students receiving intervention at a particular grade level are not making a sufficient rate of progress with the intervention instruction provided, there is a systemic problem to address first before tackling any individual teacher or student difficulties.

If the rate of progress for the grade level is insufficient, then some aspect of the intervention needs to change. If groups are meeting only three times a week, then try five times a week for the next 6 weeks and reexamine. Maybe the amount of time per day should increase from 20 to 30 minutes. If the intervention time is limited because the team is relying on the reading teachers to provide all the group instruction, then the principal needs to let the grade-level team know that for students to make more improvement, the classroom teachers also need to meet with intervention groups. Try an approach in which the reading specialist meets daily with the lowest-performing students and the classroom teacher meets with the students whose skills are not quite as far behind. If an adequate amount of instructional time was provided but the progress is insufficient, then explore some other factors. Discuss whether the group size is too large, the instruction is not focused enough, or the curriculum doesn't match the student needs well enough.

DECISIONS THAT REQUIRE PROGRESS MONITORING DATA

Moving Students From Tier II to Tier III

Some experts recommend a system in which teachers schedule periodic data meetings to discuss student progress and to determine movement of students between the tiers. In the University of Texas Center for Reading and Language Arts publication called *The 3-Tier Reading Model*, the recommendation is that students remain in Tier II for 10–12 weeks of instruction at a time. After the first round of Tier II, teachers review progress monitoring data to determine whether the student will receive another round of Tier II instruction or be moved to Tier III.

I recommend the following:

- Start most students in Tier II to see whether it works.
- Place a limited number of students immediately in Tier III if there are sufficient data to believe they will make progress only with the intensity provided in Tier III.
- Keep a student in Tier II long enough to give the instruction a chance to work.
- Move a student from Tier II to Tier III after every adjustment to Tier II has been made and the student's skills still haven't responded adequately.
- Require a minimum of three data points to compare progress with the targetline.
- Increase the frequency of progress monitoring if the student's scores are extremely variable.
- Remain flexible about when to move students.
- View the tiers as gradations along the continuum of intensity rather than only two distinct layers.

When the groups are first formed in the fall, don't be alarmed if there is a brief shake-out period during the first week when a few students need to be moved right away. Occasionally the assessment data do not accurately measure a particular student's skill level because some students are not comfortable in testing situations and others are lucky guessers.

After this initial shifting, the groups probably can remain the same for the first 6–9 weeks. If progress monitoring is assessed every 3 weeks, at week nine the initial benchmark plus three progress monitoring points will be available. If groups began meeting the third week in September, then the sixth week will be around Halloween, and the ninth week will be around Thanksgiving. Many schools more formally reexamine student progress between Halloween and Thanksgiving and then again just after the winter benchmark in January. For a student whose rate of progress is seriously insufficient, it's important not to wait too long before intensifying instruction.

> *For a student whose rate of progress is seriously insufficient, it's important not to wait too long before intensifying instruction.*

Responding to Inadequate Rates of Progress

If a student's progress is insufficient after the first round of Tier II instruction, it is tempting to move him or her immediately from Tier II to Tier III. Yet many other things can be tried first. Tier III intervention is very costly and should be the last resort.

If a student is not making adequate progress in Tier II, there are a number of alternative approaches. If the student is making progress but the rate of progress is insufficient, first try adding more time. Monitor progress weekly for 3 weeks and look at the graph again. If additional time increases the rate of progress, continue with the added time. If the rate of progress doesn't respond to additional time, then try intensifying the instruction in one of several ways. Options for intensifying instruction include the following:

- Increase the number of student responses in a minute by reducing the group size.
- Increase the number of questions and error corrections the student receives in a minute.
- Increase the scaffolding by breaking the task down more or providing more structure so that the student can be successful.
- Spend more time modeling the "I do" and "We do" guided practice before the student practices independently.

- Increase the number of repetition cycles on each skill before moving on to see whether mastery is achieved with more practice.
- Use a more systematic curriculum so that skills are taught in a prescribed manner, with the teacher asking questions and cueing with the same language for each routine.

If the student still doesn't make gains after these efforts to intensify instruction within Tier II, it may be time to move him or her to Tier III.

Determining When a Student Meets Exit Criteria

Once students receiving intervention instruction reach benchmark, it is important to exit them from Tier II or Tier III to make sure they sustain this level using only Tier I instruction and without the extra support of the intervention group. Many schools establish an exit criterion, such as a given number of progress monitoring scores at or above benchmark. The Heartland Group in Iowa recommends four data points above benchmark, and we typically advise three consecutive data points at or above benchmark.

> Once students receiving intervention instruction reach benchmark, it is important to exit them from Tier II or Tier III to make sure they sustain this level using only Tier I instruction and without the extra support of the intervention group.

Exiting students who have reached benchmark leaves more staff time and energy to focus on the students who have not responded to instruction so far. Some people call these students "treatment resisters," but this term sounds as if the students aren't cooperative. I prefer to discuss these students as those who have made an insufficient level of progress. The key word is *insufficient* because although most students respond somewhat to intensive intervention instruction, teachers should remain focused on getting each student to a sufficient level of progress. *Sufficient* is defined as progress at or above the targetline on the student's progress monitoring graph. If the progress is less than this, then the teaching staff must do everything possible to achieve a sufficient rate of progress. Remember, teachers should be striving for 95% or more of K–3 students reading at grade level. Principals

> The key word is insufficient because although most students respond somewhat to intensive intervention instruction, teachers should remain focused on getting each student to a sufficient level of progress. Sufficient is defined as progress at or above the targetline on the student's progress monitoring graph.

help when they continue to articulate the 95% goal yet accept that it may take up to 3 years to get second and third grade to that level. In many schools, more than 90% of kindergarten and first-grade students reach benchmark in the first 2 years of full RTI implementation, and 95% in kindergarten is not unusual even in the first year. Progress in second and third grade depends on first achieving high levels of benchmark in kindergarten and first grade so that fewer and fewer students reach the upper grades behind in their reading skills.

When schools fully implement tight and focused intervention group instruction just after the fall benchmark and consistently teach the groups throughout the year, rapid progress will be achieved. At least a third of the students who enter Tier II in the fall should be exited by the winter benchmark and another third by spring break. No more than one third of the students who began the year in Tier II groups should remain in a group after spring break. Generally, these groups are small, and the time for these groups is extensive.

Teachers sometimes find it difficult to exit their students from intervention groups. This reluctance may occur because these are the students they identified as struggling, and they are worried that the students will slip backwards again when removed from the intervention group. Despite any reluctance, teachers must exit the student once he or she sustains benchmark scores and then watch to make sure that he or she doesn't regress without the support of the intervention group. If a teacher keeps a student in the group without determining whether he or she can sustain the gains without the support of intervention instruction, the student will go on to the next grade-level teacher without the benefit of a closely monitored transition.

It may be easier for teachers to exit students from intervention groups if they continue monitoring the students' progress and watching their scores for at least a month after the exit. That way, if a student slips back, he or she can be placed right back in a group. If the student sustains the gain, then the teacher knows that he or she is ready for the core instruction only. When a school has universal screening of all students at the three benchmark periods per year, teachers can be assured that a student will not go more than 4 months between screenings.

USING PROGRESS MONITORING DATA AT MEETINGS

Far too often schools that implement RTI are swimming in data, yet the staff has no big-picture sense of what the data mean. Much of the time when a principal explores consulting or professional development on RTI, his or her school has been administering the CBM assessments for anywhere from 1 to 5 years. The principal typically comments that the data are not being used to inform instruction and the staff needs help learning to use the data to group students and plan intervention. One of the questions I ask, generally in the first 10 minutes of the conversation, is "Approximately what percentage of your students are at grade-level benchmark for K–3?" Most principals struggle to answer that question. It is critical for a principal to be able to name an approximate number (e.g., somewhere around 60% of the kindergartners benchmarked in DIBELS at the end of last year).

Even schools that are several years into RTI and making exceptional progress in analyzing data to make instructional decisions for each individual student are too often missing the big picture. While sitting in a kindergarten grade-level meeting recently, the team reviewed data showing that 78% of kindergartners were at benchmark in early February. When asked how that compares with last year at this same time, no one had any idea. That's a critical question for goal setting. The reading coach, who could not answer the question, had to get online and look it up. A very simple chart, like the one that follows, was needed to help the teachers consider their goal for the end of the year.

> *Far too often schools that implement RTI are swimming in data, yet the staff has no big-picture sense of what the data mean.*

Percentage of Students at Benchmark

	February	*May*
Last year	66%	89%
This year	78%	Goal needed

With this information available, a goal of 95% at benchmark this year is reasonable.

Preparing Data for Meetings

It is important to have historical and current data available to reference instantly at teacher meetings while the discussions are occurring. The RTI coordinator or coach should have a data notebook and be responsible for updating a duplicate notebook for the principal. This notebook contains copies of key data reports for the current and previous years. In addition to helping establish goals, keeping the data accessible helps avoid the spread of incorrect information.

During a recent first-grade team meeting, one resistant teacher was raising questions about why his grade team needed to implement RTI. His claim was that intervention groups weren't needed because more than 95% of first graders were at benchmark on DIBELS the previous May when baseline data were collected. Because no one at the meeting had the data handy, he swayed his colleagues to wonder why they were being asked to do this extra work.

After the meeting we checked the data, and the first-grade teacher's figure was wrong. Only 72% of students had reached benchmark on ORF and 58% in NWF. Allowing this misperception to go uncorrected during this first-grade team meeting was a huge mistake, and it affected the rest of the teachers in that meeting.

The principal needs to have two types of data readily available:

1. The percentage of students currently at benchmark at each grade level

2. Progress this year compared with the same time last year.

This information is needed not only to establish realistic goals for this year but also to help decide where to concentrate problem-solving time. For example, if the kindergarten students seem to be on track to achieve their goals this year, then it may be possible to explore whether any intervention staff can help with the students in first grade who are not as far along. If there is a dip in the percentage of students at benchmark in the middle of second grade, then that's the place to focus more of the principal's time. The principal should meet with the RTI coordinator and decide which grade-level meetings need his or her attention.

The data even show where to focus instructional attention within a grade level throughout the year. If the data show that nearly all kindergarten students reached benchmark in ISF, then the focus of the intervention groups should shift to the next skill, which is PSF. If the first graders came in with strong phonemic skills from kindergarten, then the focus of the first half of first grade should be on developing their alphabetic principle skills, as measured by the NWF indicator. If most first-grade students reached benchmark in NWF but not in ORF, then the teachers need to examine sight word acquisition and have students spend more time applying their word study skills to text.

Data Meetings With Grade-Level Teams

It is common to hear the term "data meetings" around schools that are implementing RTI. What does a data meeting look like? One type typically occurs with a grade-level team, and the purpose is to evaluate the effectiveness of the overall approach to intervention for the students at that grade level. Another is one in which all the staff that serve an individual below-benchmark student meet to analyze the student's data and discuss whether any changes in his or her intervention plan are needed.

RTI offers an opportunity to convert the discussions that occur at grade-level meetings. Too often the discussion is around administrative topics such as staffing for the field trip or deadlines for report cards. Nearly all such details can be handled via e-mail or through staff mailboxes. The grade-level meetings should be dedicated to talking about curriculum and instruction.

Some schools have changed the name of the meetings to "curriculum collaboration time" to signal that the purpose is for a team of teachers to discuss the curriculum at their grade level. Many schools provide weekly time for teams to collaborate. This is not time for teachers to make individual plans but is intended to be spent discussing curriculum with all the teachers at a grade-level meeting. It is important for the RTI coordinator to attend these meetings to facilitate communication and alignment across grade levels.

The RTI coordinator or reading coach should always bring a data notebook to these meetings. Although in some schools the grade-level team leader plans the agenda for the meeting, the RTI coordinator should have a close relationship with each team leader so that topics related to RTI are discussed at the meetings. At least monthly, the RTI coordinator should have CBM data charts ready in order to discuss the students' progress to date. RTI coordinators can update the charts by receiving the progress monitoring data from each classroom teacher. It is possible to make a fairly accurate estimate of the number of students at benchmark at any point in time from this ongoing data analysis.

After looking at progress to date, the team should discuss how the organizational structure of the intervention groups is working. Are all teachers getting in their full intervention time? Should they review the schedule of the interventionists who come into the classrooms to help teachers with a group? What materials have teachers been using that they believe are particularly effective? Is there a shortage of any materials?

Collaboration time is especially important for teams using the walk-to-intervention model, where there is an established intervention block and students receive intervention from teachers other than their homeroom teachers. As more progress monitoring data are collected, teachers may recommend that particular students in their intervention group be moved up to the next skill on the continuum. Teachers also need to review whether they have students who are not making progress and whether they should be moved down a group.

Sometimes there is a case study time during the grade-level meetings. Each week the schedule rotates, and one teacher has a total of 10 minutes on a student: 5 minutes to provide information about a student about whom they are concerned followed by 5 minutes of group brainstorming on instructional strategies to try with this student. It is helpful if the RTI coordinator provides a format for the discussion so that the teacher supplies only the pertinent data about the student during the first 5 minutes. The idea is to help teachers stay focused on data, pinpoint skill deficit areas, and analyze the success of the curriculum used so far. It is helpful if the RTI coordinator initially models what these discussions should look like so that they don't fall back into discussion about why the student's family life makes it hard for him or her to learn how to read.

The data analysis varies by time of year. At the beginning of the year, the process focuses on placing below-benchmark students in groups, and as the year progresses the discussion shifts to analyzing the progress monitoring scores to determine which students need more intensive instruction. In general, the discussion at the meetings centers around three different purposes:

- Placing below-benchmark students in groups based on skill deficits
- Determining the appropriate instructional strategies or programs for each group to address the skill deficits
- Reviewing progress monitoring data to intensify instruction for some students and to move children between groups

Data Meetings With Individual Teachers

At least every 3 months the principal and RTI coordinator should have one-on-one meetings with each teacher. The focus of these meetings is on the progress of the class overall and the progress of the individual students in the class. Each teacher should bring a data notebook to these meetings. The contents of this notebook should include the following information:

- Error pattern analysis worksheets
- Lists of intervention groups
- Progress monitoring data graphs for each below-benchmark student and each group
- Intervention logs to track attendance, intervention time per week, curriculum used each week, and observation notes on each student

One of the best reports for this meeting is available from the University of Oregon's DIBELS data management system. Similar reports may be available in other reporting systems. A sample appears in Figure B of the Case Study. This report is ideal for meetings with teachers because it shows on a single graph the level of progress at two time periods for all the students in a classroom. The principal can start by acknowledging the excellent progress made by particular students and ask the classroom teacher what she believes has caused the remarkable level of growth. Then the discussion can shift to the students not making sufficient progress.

While discussing the students who have not demonstrated a sufficient rate of progress, the principal can ask the following types of questions:

Current Intervention

- Which skills are below benchmark for this student?
- What is the most important instructional focus for this student at present?
- Which intervention group is the student in?
- What is the instructional focus of this group, and who teaches it?
- How many minutes of intervention is the student receiving per week?
- How many students are in the group with the student?

Identifying the Problem

- Is the entire group making insufficient progress, or only this student?
- How is the student's attendance?
- Would the student benefit from more time in intervention?
- Is the group too large to provide adequate corrective feedback?
- Is the focus of instruction matched to the student's core deficit?
- Does the curriculum used for the group address the student's skill deficits?
- What else have we already tried with this student?
- What other assessment data do you have for this student (e.g., results from an informal phonological or phonics assessment screening)?

Problem Solving

- Is it possible to "double-dose" this student so he or she receives intervention in two groups daily?
- Would it enhance the intervention if the parents are asked to help at home (e.g., work on a list of sight words)?
- Would moving this student to another group provide better results?
- Does this student need a different curriculum?

- What else can we provide that may help this student?
- How can the RTI coordinator help you?

Once a plan is constructed, a follow-up meeting is needed to monitor whether the changes helped. These data meetings with teachers should be focused entirely on the students and what the school community can do to create a plan to help each student reach benchmark. With the RTI coordinator in attendance, keep these discussions focused on the students, not the teacher's performance. The RTI coordinator has to remain a peer coach and cannot be placed in a position of evaluating a classroom teacher's performance.

After examining the progress of the students in a class, teachers should be asked to set a goal for the number of students they believe will reach benchmark by the end of the year. Principals can discuss this during a meeting with each teacher or provide a form to be filled out before or after the data meeting. It is helpful for each teacher to have a goal and then track the class progress toward this goal. Goal setting helps communicate accountability for the students reaching a high reading level.

Principals should be cautious about linking CBM results directly to individual teacher performance appraisals. When DIBELS or other CBM data are referenced in a teacher's performance review, there is a risk that teachers may respond by cheating on student assessments. Although it may be appropriate to say that increasing reading achievement is a goal for teachers, there are very sticky problems to deal with when the DIBELS becomes a threat to them.

Data Meetings With Parents

One of the most powerful examples of how CBM data can have a positive impact on relationships with parents comes from a principal who shared his story with his colleagues. At a quarterly meeting with four elementary principals who were implementing RTI, this principal shared an experience he had about 3 months into the first year of RTI in his school. He was meeting with a parent who was forcefully requesting that her son be moved to a different class because she feared he was not learning to read. After discovering that the parent had not yet discussed her concerns with the teacher, the principal explained that he needed to consult with the teacher about her son. The teacher joined the meeting with her RTI data notebook under her arm. The principal asked the teacher to share information about the student's assessment data and the school's plan to help raise the child's reading level.

The teacher told the parent about her child's DIBELS fall benchmark data and said that her son was receiving intervention in a small group with two other students on specific prereading skills he was lacking. The teacher then opened her data notebook and showed the parent her analysis of the error patterns on the child's DIBELS indicator probes, the focus of instruction for the group in which he was placed, and a brief overview of the type of strategies that were used in this group according to the group's weekly lesson plan. Then she showed the parent her child's progress monitoring chart and expressed that, with his current rate of progress, she fully expected that he would be at benchmark by the midyear DIBELS benchmark assessment. The teacher explained that the student would be exited from the skill group after three consecutive progress monitoring scores at or above benchmark, with progress monitoring for a month after that to make sure that he doesn't slip back.

The principal thanked the teacher and excused her to return to the classroom. The parent then expressed appreciation for what the school was doing to help her child learn to read and withdrew her request that the child be moved to a different class because the teacher obviously knew her child very well and had a plan in place that was working. The principal said that in his many years of administrative leadership, he had rarely seen anything quite as powerful for addressing this type of parent concern. The principal believes that the key to this parent's turnaround was the progress monitoring graphs that enabled the teacher to show in a concrete manner where the child's skills were, where he needed to be to reach benchmark, what the school was doing to help him, and when he was expected to reach the goal.

Communication with parents about RTI helps develop strong home–school relationships. Many schools send letters home at the beginning of RTI implementation to provide an overview of the initiative. The letters often include a parent-friendly description of what the various assessment measures mean. At an administrator workshop, one principal shared her regrets about sending home a letter for a parent's signature to gain permission to place a student in a Tier II intervention group. This permission letter raised many questions and concerns about whether the child was entering a special education procedure. The principal regretted this approach because placement in the group was delayed by several weeks. A better approach may be to explain to parents in the handbook and in communication that the school's curriculum in early reading includes periodic assessments and the use of tiered intervention instruction.

On occasion, concerns have arisen because some parents download the oral reading passages to help their child practice reading the passages. This is an unfortunate misunderstanding of the purpose of the assessment. Parents should want their child to be assessed properly because they may not be selected to receive special help if they reach benchmark levels artificially. It is important to explicitly state to parents that not practicing for the assessment is important because the norms were derived from cold reads.

DATA CHARTS THAT ARE A MUST FOR PRINCIPALS

Earlier in this chapter it was recommended that the principal and RTI coordinator have an administrative RTI data notebook. The contents will be different from the teacher's data notebooks. Resource A, at the end of this book, provides a sample set of reports for this notebook.

Effective Models of Professional Development

As a first-year teacher I have learned so much about differentiated instruction that I was never taught in college, not even on the graduate level. This program is awesome!

—Interventionist

RTI is a complex change process that involves much more than learning to analyze assessment data. Once a principal decides to implement RTI in a school, a plan for professional development (PD) is needed. The format of the school's PD is important in providing staff with the support they will need to learn about data-driven differentiated instruction. Once the administrative team makes a commitment that RTI will become a permanent part of the processes of the school, the PD plan has to match this long-term view. Workshops can provide an overview of what RTI is and how it can be beneficial for the school. Once the school decides to implement RTI, a much more comprehensive plan for PD is needed.

DESIGNING AN EFFECTIVE APPROACH TO PROFESSIONAL DEVELOPMENT

Which models of PD are most effective? Because RTI is a complex change process that involves many staff members in a school, PD should be provided in strands to meet the diverse needs of administrators, RTI coaches, and teachers.

A Sustained and Job-Embedded PD Model

Research on PD models indicates that sustained, job-embedded, long-term approaches are the most effective for supporting change in schools. Workshops can help in introducing new ideas to educators and presenting simple ideas that can be implemented with very little explanation. However, implementing RTI is not simple, and a one-shot workshop will not result in full-scale RTI implementation in a school. When the change involves a paradigm shift that affects many staff members, a single workshop doesn't provide a forum or the time for the level of dialogue teachers need to process the ideas and plan the implementation.

Planning Different Formats

A PD plan for RTI anticipates a combination of formats, including workshops, grade-level team meetings, quarterly meetings with administrators, and follow-up one-on-one coaching of the teachers as they learn how to change the intensity of instruction. At the beginning of the process, workshops can provide the same overview information about RTI to large groups within the school. Workshops can also be effective for presenting the analytical techniques teachers will need for working with student data.

> A PD plan for RTI anticipates a combination of formats, including workshops, grade-level team meetings, quarterly meetings with administrators, and follow-up one-on-one coaching of the teachers as they learn how to change the intensity of instruction.

After an initial round of workshops, the remainder of the PD for RTI ideally will be delivered by grade level and in smaller groups. Grade-level meetings are most useful for reinforcing new processes and procedures taught in larger workshops and for dialogue and collaborative planning. A coach or coordinator must be present at grade-level meetings to offer support, answer questions, communicate relevant information back to the principal, and coordinate between the grade levels. Collaboration is critical when grade-level teams select an appropriate delivery model for organizing small-group intervention instruction. Some teams decide that each teacher will teach all his or her own students, whereas other grade levels determine that students will benefit from tighter groups if the teachers share students across classrooms. Smaller discussions are also useful after teachers have begun using the analytical techniques and have questions for an expert. After Tier II instruction begins, grade-level meetings are critical for teachers. The team can examine grade-level progress and share experiences about lessons and strategies that are and are not working. At critical points in the learning process, it may be effective for teachers to bring case studies about individual students to share at grade-level team meetings.

Other PD can be delivered in individual meetings between teachers and coaches, coordinators, or outside consultants. Coaching, conferencing, and mentoring are all formats that meet the various needs of individual teachers. After the initial analytical techniques are taught in workshops and reviewed in grade-level team meetings, the one-on-one form of PD is most effective because teachers are at such different points of implementation. Some teachers assimilate this information quickly and are ready for the next step, whereas other teachers still are struggling to understand how to determine specific skill deficits by analyzing student error patterns. The best way to help teachers embrace these new practices and processes is to meet them where they are and take them to the next step. This prevents teachers who are early adopters from getting bored because the PD is too repetitious and the later-adopting teachers from tuning out because they can't ask questions and get clarification when needed.

Who Should Attend PD

The schools that have achieved the greatest gains have provided PD to several audiences, including classroom teachers, special education teachers, and Title I teachers. Title I teachers often have not received much PD, yet they are the ones working with some of the lowest-performing students. If instructional aides are going to be teaching some of the intervention groups, you may want to consider them for PD as well.

CONTENT OF PROFESSIONAL DEVELOPMENT

Customizing the content of RTI PD for each school, based on the prior knowledge and instructional skills of the teachers, keeps the staff better engaged. The success of RTI depends on the knowledge and expertise of the school's teachers. Teachers need a strong background in the essential components of reading instruction, the skills good readers exhibit, the ability to identify what poor readers lack, and a working knowledge about what good instructional practices look like. To the extent that the staff doesn't have this background knowledge, the PD for RTI must include it.

There is often confusion about the difference between program training and nonprogram PD in core skills. Program-related PD trains teachers to use a published program their school has purchased. This training typically is offered when a school adopts a new reading program and is generally taught by consultants. The training includes showing teachers how their reading program is organized, providing an overview of a single day's lesson and the layout of a weekly plan for lessons, and demonstrating the important instructional routines used in the program. Teachers report that much of the training day is devoted to learning how to navigate the materials, establishing appropriate pacing, and identifying which sections are essential and which can be skipped.

PD in core skills includes the following types of information:

- The criteria that define scientifically based reading research
- The research-validated components of effective reading instruction
- Phonological awareness skills arranged on a continuum from simple to complex
- Instructional strategies to teach students to isolate a single phoneme and strategies such as "move-it-and-say-it" to teach students to segment all the phonemes in a word
- The components of an effective phonics lesson plan
- Instructional techniques to teach students to blend sounds and read whole words
- Recognizing when to move from additive to cumulative blending techniques while teaching students the alphabetic principle
- The difference between word chains and word sorts, and when to use each technique
- The purpose and uses of various types of text, including predictable, decodable, and authentic text
- Approaches to determine when a student has mastered word reading skills and is ready for fluency
- The strategies for teaching fluency that are most effective

> *Investing in core skill PD pays in the long run because teachers will be more effective using materials and programs when they have a broader understanding of reading instruction.*

In the past, nonprogram core skill training has been lacking. Investing in core skill PD pays in the long run because teachers will be more effective using materials and programs when they have a broader understanding of reading instruction.

In addition to establishing core knowledge about effective reading instruction, teachers need other information specific to reading intervention and RTI. This includes a brief overview of research that demonstrates the effectiveness of early intervention, along with information about how early literacy assessment screening accurately identifies which children are at risk for later difficulties. An overview of the three-tier reading model is also useful so that teachers have a common language for discussing Tier I, Tier II, and Tier III.

RTI PD focuses on helping teachers learn to interpret assessment data to identify skill deficits. Generally, elementary teachers have not had a lot of experience with assessment data analysis. They are accustomed to using summative data such as the reading basal end-of-unit tests or weekly spelling tests, both of which measure whether a student mastered what was taught. Learning to use screening data in a diagnostic manner is entirely different, and elementary teachers usually are unfamiliar with this process. Teachers benefit from a specific process to follow until they develop an intuitive sense of how to observe the error patterns in a student's test probe. In learning to analyze data, teachers need not only an initial introduction in a workshop setting but also follow-up coaching and mentoring as they learn to dig deeply into the data and draw out observations about the skills the student does and does not possess.

> *In learning to analyze data, teachers need not only an initial introduction in a workshop setting but also follow-up coaching and mentoring as they learn to dig deeply into the data and draw out observations about the skills the student does and does not possess.*

DELIVERING PROFESSIONAL DEVELOPMENT IN STRANDS

Because RTI implementation affects and involves so many different kinds of staff, the needs of the various staff can best be met with separate strands of PD. There are three different types of participants, and their needs are all unique. The three audiences are administrators, reading coaches or RTI coordinators, and teachers.

Administrator Training

This training is targeted primarily for principals, but it's advisable to also include the district curriculum coordinators for reading, special education, and Title I. Before a district launches into this initiative, principals need a strong understanding of the principles behind RTI and possible motivations to consider making this change in a school. At the first overview meeting the topics include an explanation of what RTI is, the research base behind it, the three-tier reading model, and what results principals can expect if they implement this.

After principals are on board and have agreed to support RTI, a much more nuts-and-bolts session follows, with a focus not only on the events and activities but also on what to expect. Some possible topics are as follows:

- Articulating a clear and concise motivation for RTI in your school
- Developing an assessment plan that specifies who will administer the assessments
- Creating an assessment calendar with benchmark windows and periodic progress monitoring assessments
- Conducting meetings with grade-level teams to choose a delivery model for intervention groups
- Defining the role of an RTI coordinator or coach and criteria for selecting the best candidate
- Establishing procedures for placing students in groups and selecting appropriate curricula
- Monitoring the effectiveness of the three tiers through assessment walls and compiling progress monitoring data between benchmark windows
- Conducting data meetings with teachers individually and at grade level
- Setting goals for the percentage of students at benchmark at each grade level

In the most successful implementations, an ongoing series of quarterly implementation meetings is scheduled in which principals have an opportunity to share information with colleagues and to raise questions and seek advice from an RTI consultant. These meetings should be small and intimate to allow sharing of challenges and successes between principals. If the meeting is expanded to include too many other participants, the honest dialogue about the challenges is less likely to occur. The recommended list of participants includes principals, RTI coordinators or reading coaches, and one district coordinator for the initiative.

Training for RTI Coordinators and Reading Coaches

Some schools have a reading coach whose role is defined by Reading First or the district office. Schools that don't have a reading coach often create a position so there is someone designated to coordinate the RTI effort. The role of a coach or a coordinator may be quite different.

Train the RTI coordinators or reading coaches before training the teachers so that they can support their colleagues in the use of data and instruction planning. Advise the coordinator or coach to select at least one teacher per grade level who is willing and able to become an early adopter and a success story. For this early adopter, select a teacher who not only is enthusiastic about RTI but also is a very capable teacher who will easily learn to teach small groups. Your goal is to have at least one classroom at each grade level that is a model by the end of the first year.

Occasionally coaches believe that they need to concentrate their time on the teacher whose instruction needs the most improvement. Sometimes this can be a new teacher or a veteran whose teaching methods are not effective for the school's current student population. There will be plenty of time later to support the less effective teachers. At this early stage, select teachers who are good teachers and who are flexible and willing to accept suggestions from a peer coach.

Sometimes district staff members ask whether a training-of-trainers (TOT) or turnkey model is possible. The notion is to provide training for coaches or selected teachers who then turn around and provide training to their colleagues. Although this may be cost effective, TOT models often see limited success in the PD for RTI. It seems that the new trainees have not had the depth of knowledge and experience to redeliver the training appropriately. TOT models can work for some aspects, including training in how to administer and score the assessments. However, learning to use data to make decisions about students is too complex for coaches to be placed immediately in the position as a trainer. Allow them to learn by coaching the early adopters first.

The training for coaches and coordinators includes learning techniques for analyzing student testing probes, procedures for placing students in intervention groups, and approaches to creating intervention lesson plans. Four steps to learn are as follows:

- Identifying specific skill deficits for each below-benchmark student through data analysis procedures
- Placing students in small groups homogeneously by skill deficits
- Articulating a precise instructional focus for each group
- Selecting the appropriate programs, materials, or strategies for each group

After working for the first year under the guidance of someone who has experience in implementing RTI, some coaches are prepared to deliver PD on the techniques for data-informed RTI instruction.

Teacher Training

Deliver the teacher's strand of PD in stages. During the first year of implementation of RTI, the first stage is an introduction to RTI, which can occur in a meeting of approximately 2–3 hours. The topics include an overview of RTI and the research base behind it, the three-tier reading model, and a preview of some alternative ways a grade-level team might organize to deliver the small-group differentiated instruction. This can be viewed as an RTI kickoff.

After the kickoff, most schools train either an assessment team or all teachers in how to administer and score the early literacy assessments. This training is best scheduled just before teachers begin administering the assessments, so they won't forget the scoring rules. After the initial benchmark assessment, the next step is to train teachers in data analysis techniques and to learn how to dig below the score. Teachers need support in how to look beyond the instructional recommendation levels of benchmark, strategic, or intensive to discover specific student skill deficits. This training is most meaningful when teachers can use their own student data and learn how to place students in groups based on skill deficit areas. Once all below-benchmark students are placed in groups, teachers learn how to select materials, programs, or instructional strategies to use with each intervention group.

Because much of the success of RTI depends on how teachers at a grade level organize to provide the small intervention groups, meeting with grade-level teams for these discussions is most productive. It is ideal to facilitate these discussions at the individual building level. Organizing the delivery model, placing students in groups, and planning instruction all require support and follow-up.

DIFFERENTIATING THE TRAINING THROUGHOUT IMPLEMENTATION

When launching RTI, a workshop setting is fine for providing information and training in techniques for data analysis. Yet before too long it becomes evident that different teachers have progressed at different rates. After about 8 weeks of intervention groups, the teachers are all at different stages of implementation. Some have understood what to do and are off and running. Others are still very confused about how to focus their instruction and cannot figure out how to look at a student probe and pinpoint the student's key skill deficits.

During a full-day workshop in late September for five kindergarten teachers, the participants went through an overview of data analysis techniques, approaches for grouping, and an overview of lesson planning. During the first follow-up visit around Halloween, the kindergarten teachers were already at different points. Two younger teachers who are friends outside school had worked together to talk through their students' data, and they had prepared some phonemic awareness materials and were teaching small groups daily. By the time we returned they had monitored their students' progress and had very specific and informed questions about how to refine their instruction. One of these teachers talked about a student she had retained last year, and she said that if she had known then what she knows now, she would not have retained the student.

Although two of the kindergarten teachers had made tremendous progress in embracing the ideas and putting the procedures into practice, the other three teachers at this grade level were not at the same point. It was clear when they raised concerns about what was developmentally appropriate that the other three teachers were not teaching small groups much. They spoke about teaching letter naming to all their groups because that was what they had always done, even when the data showed that some of the students didn't need more instruction in that area. Once it became clear that there was such variation in teacher readiness, we split the grade-level meeting into two groups and proceeded with different content and pacing for each group. For the three teachers, we had to revisit the procedures for using the data to place students in small groups by skill deficit areas and reiterate that differentiated instruction means that not all the groups get the same lesson plan.

At a different school, the first follow-up visit revealed that there was minimal student improvement because too little time was devoted to intervention groups. At the kindergarten grade-level meeting, the teachers were asked to place their student booklets in two groups based on whether the students were making adequate or inadequate progress. When the pile representing students making insufficient progress was much larger, it was clear that there was a systemic problem. That insight determined the direction of the next few questions in the meeting. How many times a week do the intervention groups meet? How long do the groups meet each time? It turned out that the teachers were relying solely on the reading specialist to meet with all the intervention groups. Because she was serving groups from six grade levels, she was meeting with the kindergarten intervention groups for only about 10 minutes twice a week. This is not enough time, so the team had to collaborate to solve the systemic problem first.

Anticipate from the start that the PD will vary because teachers will need different things at different points along the way. Sometimes the coordinator may need to plan a "make and take" to get beyond objections about not having time to make activities for intervention groups. Other times a grade-level team will need to stop and figure out how they can change the schedule to make intervention work more smoothly for everyone. Other times the meeting format may have to encourage teachers to share their successes. Some modest teachers won't share because they feel this would be bragging. Establish a process that encourages sharing so that great ideas can surface more comfortably.

The following is a list of ways to get teachers going with their implementation of intervention groups:

- Provide classroom release time just after benchmark testing to make it easier for teachers to have time to group students and plan intervention lessons.
- Facilitate a grade-level discussion about materials to use for intervention groups.
- Provide training on one intervention program, such as Road to the Code (Blachman, Ball, Black, & Tangel, 2000) for kindergarten staff.
- Provide copies of student center activities from the Florida Center for Reading Research.
- Organize intervention binders with a tab for each deficit skill area.
- Share a list of favorite activities per skill.
- Purchase some packaged kits to save time and demonstrate how to use them.
- Plan a "make and take" so teachers leave with activities prepared and catalogued according to the skills addressed.
- Share copies of lesson plans.

DEALING WITH RELUCTANT OR RESISTANT TEACHERS

Some teachers are simply reluctant or resistant to RTI implementation. There is a difference between these two behaviors. Reluctant teachers may just need more time, information, or support. To get the reluctant teachers to implement, principals probably need to spend a lot of time explaining why RTI is what the school needs to do. Much of this dialogue happens behind the scenes and not necessarily at meetings.

Resistant teachers have the information they need but are actively or passively not implementing intervention groups in the recommended approach. Motivate the resisters by going back to the student data and comparing their classroom's lack of growth with those making progress. Individual discussions with resistant teachers should focus on why there is a lack of student progress and what must be different. At some point a principal has to be willing to make some staff members angry, if necessary, and move the uncooperative teachers out of the way if they make it clear that they don't want to get on board.

Working hard to make RTI a part of the school's culture will help. It also helps if the principal isn't the only leader of the initiative. This initiative cannot center on the principal or one charismatic leader. RTI processes and practices have to be so

> *RTI processes and practices have to be so embedded in the school that if a principal moves to another job, RTI continues regardless of who sits in the principal's chair.*

embedded in the school that if a principal moves to another job, RTI continues regardless of who sits in the principal's chair.

SHARING EARLY SUCCESS STORIES

When principals are asked to describe some of the most important factors in their school's implementation of RTI, the conversation always includes a discussion of the success stories. One of the most powerful ways to promote a school's implementation is for the entire staff to observe the increase in student scores. The reluctant teachers generally become convinced to join in when the students in a neighboring class are improving more than their own students. Generally, at kindergarten the successes become evident quickly, even before the winter benchmark. Progress monitoring is an important way to identify the successes before January. Success stories will become the principal's most powerful tool for helping teachers who are not implementing fully.

What the Future Holds for RTI

RTI has gained acceptance as a paradigm that makes sense, and many schools have moved beyond needing to be convinced of the rationale to the implementation phase. At the time this book was written, most principals were ready to implement and seeking information about what it looks like and how to get started. The topics covered in this book were selected to help principals in the early processes of planning and implementing RTI in their school.

The future is likely to include resolution of a couple of issues that consistently emerge for schools involved in the early stages of RTI implementation. The first topic is the interpretation of the three-tier reading model as a model to be followed rigidly versus a descriptive framework to help schools launch reading instruction. The second is the role of purchased programs as curricula for intervention groups.

Two other areas will be interesting to observe in the future of RTI. As schools implement RTI, the role of special education is likely to continue to emerge. Finally, how will a school's implementation of RTI in early reading broaden to other grade levels and other disciplines? It's likely that most schools will start implementing RTI at K–3 in reading and then expand to middle school and high school. Not only will the expansion occur in later grades for reading, but schools will want to use the same approach in math and other discipline areas.

THREE-TIER MODEL AS DESCRIPTIVE, NOT PRESCRIPTIVE

As the staff in a school begins to visualize what RTI might look like when fully implemented, the three-tier model is helpful. At the beginning of implementation, the staff needs a framework for thinking about how to organize instruction in tiers to meet the needs of all students, and the three-tier model has served that purpose. It provides a set of terms and a new language for speaking about whether a student in Tier II is making sufficient progress and about when to move students to the more intensive Tier III.

Despite its usefulness as a framework, too many schools see the three-tier reading model as prescriptive rather than descriptive. As many schools try to implement RTI and follow the three tiers of instruction, they are struggling to define the processes. In that struggle, they are looking for advice, particularly the recommendations in the publication from the Vaughn Gross Center for Reading and Language Arts (2005). This publication recommends that students be in the first round of Tier II for 10–12 weeks, and then there is a decision point at which a team determines whether the student should remain in Tier II for a second round of another 10–12 weeks. Charts in the publication suggest the number of minutes of intervention for each tier and the type of curriculum that might be appropriate.

Although Sharon Vaughn clearly states that these recommendations are descriptive, some schools are tempted to implement these suggestions rigidly. The definition of the tiers of instruction is useful merely as a starting point for discussing RTI. The best implementations of RTI occur when the leaders begin with a more fluid view of the tiers. Evaluations to determine when to provide more intensive instruction can occur throughout the first 10 weeks of instruction. After three progress monitoring points, it is often clear whether the student is making sufficient progress. Schools cannot afford to wait to make adjustments. It is better to ensure that teachers who are instructing Tier II groups are using increasingly more scaffolding and more systematic modeling procedures when needed. The characteristics of instruction that are useful in Tier III can be applied in a Tier II group as needed.

The notion of checkpoints to review the data for all students placed in intervention groups is useful when RTI is first implemented. The benefit is that it articulates a process whereby teachers collaborate to check on the progress monitoring data and make decisions about which students are ready to exit groups, participate in their intervention for another round, or move to a group where instruction is more intensive. After the staff begins to implement RTI, moving students between the tiers also is a more fluid process. There is no reason to wait to reach checkpoints. Teachers learn to examine their data continuously as each progress monitoring point is added to the targetline graph, and they know when a student's lack of progress means that it's time to try a different approach.

APPROPRIATE USE OF PROGRAMS

Educational publishers are rushing to release products in the hot market of intervention materials. More than 200 programs are available today, marketed specifically for use in providing small-group intervention instruction to below-benchmark students. Schools are confused about which programs to use for what purposes. Should the programs cover all five essential components of reading instruction? What is the difference between a program for Tier II and Tier III groups? Is it better to provide teachers with programs, or should teachers create their own lessons for some of their groups? How can a school tell whether a program is research based and effective for their population of students?

In the implementation of Reading First, some state departments of education have attempted to clarify these questions for funded schools. Some states have established lists of qualified intervention programs from which schools can select, and others have encouraged schools to evaluate the materials themselves and defend their selections. The University of Oregon and the Florida Center for Reading Research have published evaluations of programs, which can be found online. Keeping these evaluations current as new materials were released was very difficult. The University of Oregon produced a rubric for evaluating and scoring the attributes of a program called *Consumer's Guide to Evaluating a Core Reading Program.*

Some books include lists of recommended programs, although this book intentionally does not. There are many problems with providing evaluations or recommendations of programs. First, it's nearly impossible to recommend intervention programs without knowing quite a bit about the core program the school uses, the data describing below-benchmark students, and the staff's knowledge and skills in teaching reading. Some published core programs are stronger in one component than others. When a program is already strong in teaching a component, then many materials can be pulled from the core for reteaching the groups that are only somewhat behind in the skill. Some core programs are weak in particular areas, such as systematic decoding instruction, or do not provide adequate emphasis on teaching and developing fluency at the text level. Some schools do not use a published basal reading program and rely instead on incidental phonics instruction within guided reading groups.

Other schools have a large English-as-a-second-language population and need to supplement vocabulary for one of the two intervention blocks.

Too many educators are searching for programs that they believe will be the silver bullet that will solve all their students' reading problems. Programs and materials do help save teachers time. With a less knowledgeable teaching staff, strong scripted programs can raise the level of instruction somewhat. Schools can achieve some improvement by purchasing strong programs with specified lesson plans and instructing teachers to use the programs for all their groups. However, the results possible with this approach are limited. Not all students will reach benchmark with the use of a protocol approach in which all groups are placed in programs that are meant to serve all below-benchmark students, as if all groups have the same needs.

> *Too many educators are searching for programs that they believe will be the silver bullet that will solve all their students' reading problems.*

First, the pacing is too slow or too fast for some students. Second, the skills covered are right only for a specific number of students and too broad for the gap kids, who have mastered some skills but not others.

The best approach for a school is to purchase a few key intervention materials. It may be effective to purchase a program that is used for Tier III groups, where the students are very far behind in all skills. Many of these more comprehensive programs include some degree of instruction in phonological awareness (and can be supplemented where needed), phonics, and word pattern skills taught in a sequential and systematic manner. Fluency is also addressed to some degree. When the programs also dedicate time to vocabulary and comprehension instruction during intervention, it tends to cut down the time dedicated to word skills. It may be better to provide a separate intervention block of time on vocabulary than to take time away from the focus of phonics and word study. Children need to receive their comprehension instruction during the core time. It takes the entire 30 minutes or more to teach an effective phonics and word study lesson in which adequate time is spent on transferring the skills taught in isolation to successfully reading the words in the context of decodable text. The more skills covered in the intervention lesson, the less time available for a strong, explicit teaching of the decoding skills. The best Tier II intervention programs focus on a limited skill area rather than trying to cover all five essential components in every intervention lesson. It is impossible to teach well the five skills in a 30-minute intervention lesson when it takes 90 minutes during the core to cover them.

Programs are only as good as the teachers who teach them, and this is never more true than in the area of intervention. Effective intervention instruction is characterized by teachers who know when to vary the program's lesson plan. The very nature of intervention instruction is that it is differentiated and that the teacher reteaches the concept if the student doesn't demonstrate mastery during the "you do" practice, after a strong "I do" and "we do" component.

Schools may benefit from listing all the materials and programs they currently have, organizing them into an intervention toolkit chart, and identifying any areas where purchasing more materials makes sense. Phonological awareness can be

> *Programs are only as good as the teachers who teach them, and this is never more true than in the area of intervention.*

taught easily with materials and activity books. Fluency requires the purchase of passages that are leveled, and many programs are good and not overly expensive. Fewer students need comprehension instruction, and many times teachers know the most about teaching comprehension strategies. The comprehension materials available also are not overly expensive. The costly programs are the ones that provide materials for teaching phonics and word study skills. This is where it is worth purchasing materials because they are the hardest for teachers to create.

The school may need two different phonics programs for intervention. The first one may be for Tier III and is a very systematic and sequential program that will be followed from the first lesson to the last for the students who are missing nearly every skill area. The second kind is helpful for the Tier II groups and organized in such a way that individual sets of lessons can be pulled by skill area. For example, a series of lessons to teach the long vowel, silent *e* pattern can be used for some groups, while other teachers pull the lessons related to short vowels. Many schools place these lesson materials in bags so that teachers can check out a bag corresponding to one phonics skill for the week. Copies of additional decodable text for students to practice can be placed in these bags as well.

FUTURE OF SPECIAL EDUCATION CURRICULUM IN READING

Once struggling readers receive Tier II and Tier III instruction in general education that is focused, explicit, and data driven, how will the curriculum provided in special education change to respond to this new breed of students? Presumably the students who qualify to receive services on an Individualized Education Plan (IEP) will

> *Presumably the students who qualify to receive services on an Individualized Education Plan (IEP) will enter special education after having received more explicit and focused instruction than ever delivered in general education.*

enter special education after having received more explicit and focused instruction than ever delivered in general education. What instruction will special education teachers provide that will help these insufficient responders read successfully?

Schools that have implemented an RTI approach to early reading have seen smaller numbers of students qualifying for special education. If special education teachers have smaller numbers of students to serve, how can this scenario create an opportunity to organize in ways never before done? Will the curricula used to teach the students who made an insufficient rate of progress in Tiers II and III be different in special education? Do special education teachers have the training, materials, and techniques necessary to teach a smaller group of students who have significantly greater difficulty?

Will the curriculum-based measures used to progress monitor in Tiers II and III affect assessment practices in special education? In one special education cooperative in Kansas, all special education teachers have been trained to use Dynamic Indicators of Basic Early Literacy Skills (DIBELS) and informal phonological awareness and phonics diagnostic screening instruments. Special education teachers in the cooperative are creating curriculum-based targetlines for students on IEPs and measuring progress periodically, just as classroom teachers do for students in Tier II and Tier III. If a student on an IEP is reading 2 years below grade level, the cooperative has defined a process to assess him at his reading level with an expected increase to grade level over time. The teacher draws a targetline on a progress monitoring chart first in passages 2 years behind, then another line for passages 1 year behind, and then a third line to measure progress in passages at grade level.

Schools need special education teachers to be the most knowledgeable ones in the school on techniques to use for students who aren't responding to reading instruction. It is easy to see special education teachers as a resource for general education teachers and intervention teachers. What is more difficult is to know what steps are needed to help every special education teacher receive the knowledge, training, and experience to step into the role as a resident expert on instruction for struggling readers.

BROADENING OF RTI BEYOND EARLY READING

The focus of this book is on implementing RTI in reading. Most districts implement RTI first in the early grades in elementary schools and then expand to later elementary grades. Many middle schools are already trying to implement RTI to address the serious reading deficits of a portion of their student population. As discussed earlier in this book, RTI implementation in reading will be different in middle school than on the elementary level. The schedule must be arranged to provide 2 hours of reading instruction for below-benchmark students, and it is likely that only a few teachers will provide this intervention rather than training all teachers to be interventionists, as in elementary school. Even after full RTI implementation in the elementary schools reduces the number of students reaching middle school below benchmark in reading, there will always be a need for reading intervention to serve students who move into the district and didn't benefit from earlier intervention.

The future for RTI in reading is to address how to serve struggling high school students. The issues are even more challenging than in middle school because the later the intervention is provided, the more difficult the process of reaching grade level in reading. What will it take to bring high school students to grade level? What structures must be in place in our schools to serve students who are reading seriously below expectations? How can we determine curricula that work while also addressing motivation and self-esteem problems? What curricula and teacher training will be needed?

In addition to expanding to other grade levels in reading, RTI is likely to spread to use in math and other discipline areas. Tiers of instruction to meet the needs of students are not difficult to visualize for any discipline. Effective early screening and diagnostic assessments are needed. The screening assessments identify which students are struggling, diagnostic assessments pinpoint which skills are deficient, and progress monitoring assessments measure increases in skills once intervention instruction begins. Because curriculum-based measurements are at the heart and soul of RTI, implementation in other disciplines must wait until the assessments are readily available. Once the assessments are available, RTI implementation in math and other disciplines is likely to proceed rapidly.

Resources

Sample Administrative RTI Data Notebook

Figure R.1 Comparison of Current Year With Previous Year DIBELS Scores by Instructional Recommendation Level

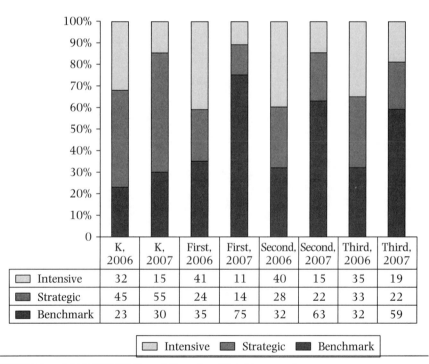

	K, 2006	K, 2007	First, 2006	First, 2007	Second, 2006	Second, 2007	Third, 2006	Third, 2007
Intensive	32	15	41	11	40	15	35	19
Strategic	45	55	24	14	28	22	33	22
Benchmark	23	30	35	75	32	63	32	59

Intensive   Strategic   Benchmark

Figure R.2 DIBELS Individual Student Performance Profile

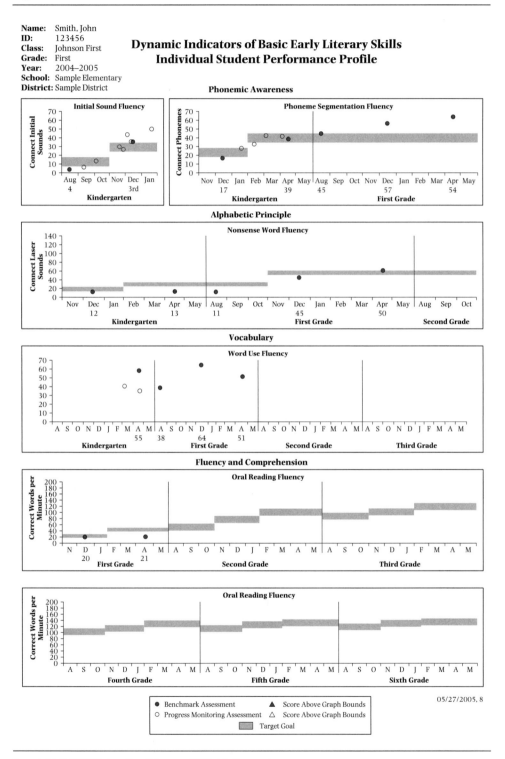

Figure R.3   Sample DIBELS Report Distribution Summary (Kindergarten)

District: Sample District
School: All Schools
Date: January, 2001–2002
Breakdown by School

Dynamic Indicators of Basic Early Literacy Skills
Kindergarten Distribution Summary

	ISF	LNF	PSF	NWF	Instructional Recommendation
Totals for district 463 students tested	Deficit: 31 (7%) Emerging: 198 (43%) Established: 233 (50%)	At Risk: 130 (28%) Some Risk: 123 (27%) Low Risk: 209 (45%)	At Risk: 48 (10%) Some Risk: 73 (16%) Low Risk: 342 (74%)	At Risk: 55 (12%) Some Risk: 109 (24%) Low Risk: 299 (65%)	Intensive: 66 (14%) Strategic: 157 (34%) Benchmark: 239 (52%) Missing Data: 1 (0%)
Adams 89 students tested	Deficit: 6 (7%) Emerging: 44 (49%) Established: 39 (44%)	At Risk: 19 (21%) Some Risk: 29 (33%) Low Risk: 41 (46%)	At Risk: 5 (6%) Some Risk: 16 (18%) Low Risk: 68 (76%)	At Risk: 9 (10%) Some Risk: 24 (27%) Low Risk: 56 (63%)	Intensive: 9 (10%) Strategic: 35 (39%) Benchmark: 45 (51%) Missing Data: 0 (0%)
Garfield 77 students tested	Deficit: 5 (6%) Emerging: 34 (44%) Established: 38 (49%)	At Risk: 29 (38%) Some Risk: 20 (26%) Low Risk: 28 (36%)	At Risk: 14 (18%) Some Risk: 17 (22%) Low Risk: 46 (60%)	At Risk: 7 (9%) Some Risk: 32 (42%) Low Risk: 38 (49%)	Intensive: 17 (22%) Strategic: 28 (36%) Benchmark: 32 (42%) Missing Data: 0 (0%)
Jefferson 69 students tested	Deficit: 3 (4%) Emerging: 24 (35%) Established: 42 (61%)	At Risk: 13 (19%) Some Risk: 12 (17%) Low Risk: 44 (64%)	At Risk: 7 (10%) Some Risk: 10 (14%) Low Risk: 52 (75%)	At Risk: 8 (12%) Some Risk: 6 (9%) Low Risk: 55 (80%)	Intensive: 7 (10%) Strategic: 16 (23%) Benchmark: 46 (67%) Missing Data: 0 (0%)
Lincoln 80 students tested	Deficit: 6 (8%) Emerging: 38 (48%) Established: 35 (44%)	At Risk: 18 (23%) Some Risk: 19 (24%) Low Risk: 42 (53%)	At Risk: 7 (9%) Some Risk: 8 (10%) Low Risk: 65 (81%)	At Risk: 14 (18%) Some Risk: 15 (19%) Low Risk: 51 (64%)	Intensive: 10 (13%) Strategic: 23 (29%) Benchmark: 46 (57%) Missing Data: 1 (1%)
Mckinley 47 students tested	Deficit: 5 (11%) Emerging: 28 (43%) Established: 22 (47%)	At Risk: 12 (26%) Some Risk: 18 (38%) Low Risk: 17 (36%)	At Risk: 6 (13%) Some Risk: 6 (13%) Low Risk: 35 (74%)	At Risk: 6 (13%) Some Risk: 12 (26%) Low Risk: 29 (62%)	Intensive: 8 (17%) Strategic: 18 (38%) Benchmark: 21 (45%) Missing Data: 0 (0%)

"Missing Data" refers to students who have been texted on some measurements for the requested assessment period, but are missing some scores that are required to determine the Instructional Recommendation.

Distributed Summary, 05/25/2004, 1

Figure R.4 Summary of Effectiveness of Core Program

Dynamic Indicators of Basic Early Literacy Skills Summary of Effectiveness of Core Program

District: Test District
School: Adams
Date: September, 2001–2002
Class: Adams K#4
Step: Beginning of Kindergarten to Middle of Kindergarten

Effectiveness of Core Curriculum

Students at Benchmark Beginning of Year	Beginning ISF Score	Middle ISF Score	Check if Reached Middle ISF Benchmark of 25
B. EMERLAD	25	60	✓
B. KAYLEE	26	32	✓
C. LEXINGTON	45	50	✓
E. CALEM	21	70	✓
G. WILLIAM	17	42	✓
H. ADRIAN	18	20	
J. AUSTIN	20	31	✓
M. JUSTIN	9	48	✓

School: Adams
Class: Adams K#4 — Count/Percent: 7/8 88%

Effectiveness of Strategic Support Program

Students at Strategic at Beginning of Year	Beginning ISF Score	Check if Reached Middle ISF Score	Middle ISF Benchmark of 25
B. CHELSEA	6	25	✓
D. KAI	14	40	✓
M. AUSTENE	23	17	
P. NYSHEL	11	23	
R. CHRISTIAN	4	9	
V. IRIS	23	30	✓
W. KATHLEEN	8	15	
W. NICHOLAS	18	28	✓
Y. SAMANTHA	10	14	

School: Adams
Class: Adams K#4 — Count/Percent: 4/9 44%

Effectiveness of Intensive Support Program

Students at Intensive Beginning of Year	Beginning ISF Score	Check if Reached Middle ISF Score	Middle ISF Benchmark of 25
B. JUDY	2	5	
D. MARIAH	5	51	✓
R. MICHAEL	0	24	

School: Adams
Class: Adams K#4 — Count/Percent: 2/3 33%

Summary of Effectiveness Report, 05/25/2004. 1

Figure R.5 Effectiveness of Tiers I, II, and III

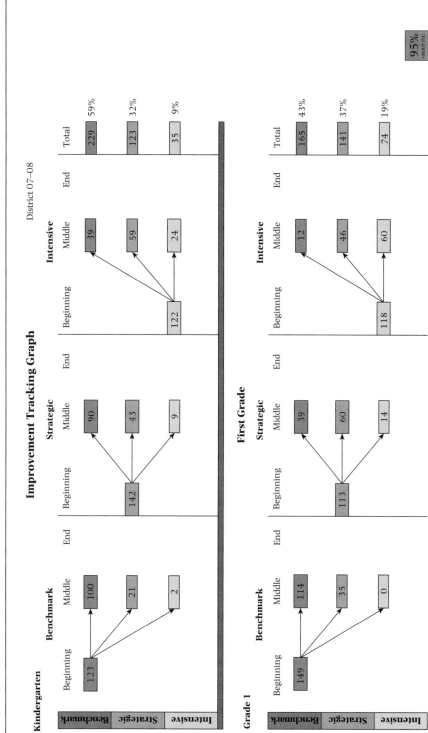

References

Blachman, B., Ball, E., Black, R., & Tangel, D. (2000). *Road to the code: A phonological awareness program for young children.* Baltimore: Paul H. Brookes.

Brown-Chidsey, R., & Steege, M. (2005). *Response to Intervention: Principles and strategies for effective practice.* New York: Guilford.

Conzemius, A., & O'Neill, J. (2001). *Building shared responsibility for student learning.* Alexandria, VA: Association for Supervision and Curriculum.

Fletcher, J. (2006, November 8). Response to Intervention Symposium, International Dyslexia Association International Conference, Indianapolis, IN.

Foorman, B. R., Fletcher, J. M., Francis, D. J., Schatschneider, C., & Mehta, P. (1998). The role of instruction in learning to read: Preventing reading failure in at-risk children. *Journal of Educational Psychology, 90*(1), 37–55.

Fuchs, L. S., & Fuchs, D. (2006a). *Progress monitoring in the context of responsiveness-to-intervention.* Retrieved January 1, 2007, from http://www.studentprogress.org/summer_institute/rti/UsingCBMDetermineRTI/UsingCBMRTI_manual.pdf

Fuchs, L. S., & Fuchs, D. (2006b). *What is scientifically-based research on progress monitoring?* Retrieved January 1, 2007, from http://www.studentprogress.org/library/What_I_%20Scientifically_based_research.rtf

Good, R. H., Gruba, J., & Kaminski, R. A. (2001). Best practices in using Dynamic Indicators of Basic Early Literacy Skills (DIBELS) in an outcomes-driven model. *Best Practices in School Psychology, 4,* 679–700.

Grimes, J., & Tilly, D. (2003). Presentation at the Innovations Conference, Charleston, SC, September 2003. Retrieved June 2, 2007, from http://www/pattan.k12.pa.us/files/SchlInterv/RtIOverview110205.pdf

Hasbrouck, J., & Denton, C. (2006). *The reading coach: A how-to manual for success.* Longmont, CO: Sopris West.

Heinzelman, D., & LaPointe, S. (2006). *Response to Intervention: Enhancing the learning of all children.* Lansing: Michigan Association of Administrators of Special Education.

Lyon, G. R. (1997, July 10). Report on learning disabilities research. Article adapted from testimony of Dr. G. Reid Lyon before the Committee on Education and Workforce, U.S. House of Representatives. Retrieved May 10, 2001, from http://www.ldonline.org/ld_indepth/reading/nih_report/html

Lyon, G. R., Fletcher, J. M., Shaywitz, B., Shaywitz, S., Torgesen, J., Wood, F., et al. (2001). Rethinking learning disabilities. In *Rethinking special education for a new century* (pp. 259–280). Washington, DC: Thomas B. Fordham Foundation/Progressive Policy Institute.

McCook, J. E. (2006). *The RTI guide: Developing and implementing a model in your schools.* Horsham, PA: LRP Publications.

National Association of State Directors of Special Education (NASDSE). (2006). *Response to Intervention: Policy considerations and implementation.* Alexandria, VA: Author.

95 Percent Group Inc. (2006). *Phonics Screener for Intervention™.* Chicago: Author. Available at http://www.95percentgroup.com

Torgesen, J. (2004, Fall). Preventing early reading failure and its devastating downward spiral: The evidence for early intervention. *American Educator, 28*(3), 6–10.

University of Oregon. (2007). *Consumer's guide to evaluating a core reading program.* Available at http://www.reading.uoregon.edu/curricula

Vaughn Gross Center for Reading and Language Arts. (2005). *Introduction to the 3-tier reading model: Reducing reading disabilities for kindergarten through third grade students* (3rd ed.). Austin, TX: Author.

Index